THE 5 PILLARS OF EFFECTIVE PUBLIC SPEAKING

THE 5 PILLARS OF EFFECTIVE PUBLIC SPEAKING

Your Unrivalled Guide to Presentation Excellence and Public Speaking Confidence

Kyle Murtagh

THE 5 PILLARS OF EFFECTIVE PUBLIC SPEAKING

Your Unrivalled Guide to Presentation Excellence
and Public Speaking Confidence

ISBN 979-8-66817-585-7

ABOUT THE AUTHOR

Kyle Murtagh is not your 'normal' Presentation Skills Coach. You see, he is about 20 years younger than the rest, has zero experience working a corporate 9-5 and is a self-confessed introvert who likes the silence of his own company. Hardly, the ideal profile for someone who is meant to be good at public speaking.

So, why bother listening to Kyle?

Well, in the last three years, he has already achieved numerous high-level public speaking accolades - including becoming a UK & Ireland Champion, 2020 - has helped hundreds of business professionals generate more leads and sales from their presentations and has inspired countless numbers to break past their crippling fear of public speaking and discover their inner confidence.

Kyle firmly believes that everyone can become a confident public speaker, as long as they are willing to put in the work, learn the acquired skills and most importantly, step outside their comfort zone and onto the public speaking stage.

Today, by purchasing this book, you have taken that first step outside your comfort zone. From this point forward you will learn a plethora of skills which, over time, will transform you into the self-assured, enthralling speaker you were meant to be.

Please share your transformations with Kyle, by using the hashtag: #5PillarsPublicSpeaking. If seen, he will actually respond!

This book is dedicated to my lovely, kind Gran.

CONTENTS

ACKNOWLEDGEMENTS

A number of people have been instrumental in guiding me as a speaker and in the creation of this paperback/audiobook.

Firstly, I must thank Greg Friel from *Frielance Music & Media*. His expertise, skills and unique sense of humour made creating the audiobook a fun, enjoyable experience which I would gladly do again.

Secondly, I must congratulate Stuart Aitken from *Aitken Design*. He truly has created remarkable artwork which I am proud to say represents this book.

Thirdly, I must express my appreciation to James McGinty (mcginty.net), who has acted as a mentor to me since I began my public speaking journey. Without a doubt he has fast-tracked my progression and I continue to learn from him to this day.

Finally, the gratitude I have for the help I received from my girlfriend, Emma Greer and my Mum, Jane Murtagh is unparalleled. From the very first draft to the day of publishing, both have committed a tremendous amount of time, effort and support which unquestionably made this book possible.
Love you both!

INTRODUCTION – YOUR FIRST STEP

When speaking in public, have you ever wished that you could put on an invisibility cloak, tiptoe past your bewildered audience, and slip out of the room without anyone noticing?

As I stood there with sweat on my brow, butterflies beating in my stomach and 40 piercing eyes staring directly at me, I really wished magic were real.

This was the first time in my adult life that I had been asked to speak in public. The venue for my baptism of fire took place in the magnificent Victorian styled Glasgow City Chambers. However, to be honest, I could barely notice its beauty. All I could think was, *"What if I freeze?","* What *if the audience don't like me?"*, *"What if they laugh at my voice?"*. *"What if What if? What if?"* ... clouded my mind.

I was visiting a Speakers Club; a place people go to practice public speaking outside their working environment. At these clubs they always encourage new people, like me, to get involved by doing something called 'Table Topics'. This ominous task involves you being asked a question on absolutely anything. From: 'What would you do if you were in power?' to 'Which do you prefer – Rice Krispies or Coco Pops?'- you just don't know

1

what is coming at you. Regardless of your knowledge, you must immediately speak on that topic for two whole minutes in front of a room full of strangers. And on that day, I will never forget the topic I was asked,

"Kyle, if a Zombie Apocalypse happened in Glasgow, where would you go?".

"...WHAT?!"

I couldn't believe it! Cue, the sweaty brow, butterflies, and thoughts of invisibility cloaks. As I stood there, frozen to the spot, with nowhere to go, one solitary, ridiculous thought popped into my mind and came out of my mouth before I had the chance to stop it.

"THE PUB!

With these two words said, I sat back down. Although, I can see how it was humorous for others, it was traumatic for me because for the first time in my life I realised I had a real, visceral fear of public speaking.

Fast forward 3 years, and I've become a UK & Ireland Public Speaking Champion, have trained and developed hundreds of business professionals all around the world and now have a fear of NOT speaking in public.

So, what has changed?

Well that day I made a decision – much like the decision you made when purchasing this book. I decided that I was going to be proactive in overcoming my fear. I was prepared to read the books, watch the videos, and most importantly, regularly step outside my comfort zone and onto the public speaking stage. Over time, I learned that there are five key skills that you need to master in order to keep your audience fully engaged, make your presentations memorable and clear, and have a significant impact.

But the real result of mastering these five skills is the unparalleled confidence it gives you when you speak in front of any size of audience – whether it be 3 or 300,000 – your confidence will remain rock solid.

These 5 skills are known as **'The 5 Pillars of Effective Public Speaking'** and I want to share them with you in this book.

However, you must understand that this book is designed with one sole purpose – for you to take action. You will learn lots about public speaking skills, about the mindset of successful speakers and how to succeed in front of any audience, but all of that will be entirely useless if you do nothing with it.

Too many of us are guilty, me included at times, of hearing a great speaker, reading a great book, receiving training from a great coach, but then doing nothing. We procrastinate – we tell ourselves, 'Tomorrow will do'. However, deep down you and I know, tomorrow will not do. It must be today; when the idea is fresh, vibrant, and raring to go. Tomorrow is simply not guaranteed; you may have great intentions, but life has a habit of unexpectedly flipping the script.

That is why when exploring this book, I recommend that you schedule at least 15 minutes of free time after your reading or listening session. That 15-minute window will give you an opportunity to immediately act on the information you have just learned. Whether that be a voice technique or a mindset change – your allocated '15 minutes of action' will help you become a more confident, captivating speaker, one step at a time.

To inspire your '15-minutes of action', at the end of each chapter there is a specific Action Point. These points will focus your learning, will encourage you to think about your own presentations, and how potentially the skills in this book could enhance your speaking. The action points listed have positively transformed the confidence and presentation skills of many of my clients. I am confident, if you take regular action, they will do the same for you.

Share on Social Media

Throughout, please document the 'actions' you take on social media by using the hashtag: - **#5PillarsPublicSpeaking.**

This will give you the opportunity to connect with others who are on the same journey as you – to become a better speaker – and will also allow you to connect with me, as I will be responding with feedback and advice to as many posts as possible – especially on LinkedIn.

What You Need to Know

Finally, I must raise the philosophy of this book. Throughout, one core truth will continuously be present, and I want you to keep it in mind as you work through each chapter. That truth is:

The success of any presentation can be determined by whether your audience act on your words or not.

This philosophy is very black and white, and you may disagree with it — which is fine! If you do, you should stop listening or reading now. But if you really think about it, the reason you are presenting in the first place is to trigger action. You want people to buy your product or service, invest in your big idea, change their habits, take your advice, move forward positively, or become inspired.

Surely, the worst possible scenario would be for you to present and for nothing to happen afterwards? That would mean you have wasted both the audience's time and your own time. Do you really want to do that?

Of course not, you want to cause action — because you want to have an impact when you speak. This book will help you do that by focusing on your **Delivery** and **Content**.

Delivery is how you convey your information. It is how you use your body language and voice to articulate your ideas, keep your audience fully engaged and stand out from the crowd.

Content, on the other hand, is your actual information. This information might come in the form of statistics, stories, or philosophies – it is the core message you are trying to project to your audience.

Here is my question: which do you think is more important? Delivery or Content?

Well, let's analyse!

You could have the most important message in the world to share, a message which could change the lives of millions. But if you deliver that message in a boring, lethargic way no one is going to listen.

Likewise, you could have absolute rubbish to say. Pure unquestionable, garbage; however, if you share it in a compelling way, people will listen, but they won't gain anything from it.

Therefore, in answering the question, both are equally important. To produce a masterclass presentation, we need high quality, engaging Delivery with powerful Content to match. The aim of this book is to show you how to achieve this high standard of presentation by providing you with the skills and techniques to enhance both your Delivery and Content.

With that in mind, let me introduce you to **THE 5 PILLARS OF EFFECTIVE PUBLIC SPEAKING**:

1. **Body Language**
2. **Voice**
3. **Structure**
4. **Clarity**
5. **Impact**

The first 2 pillars (**Body Language** and **Voice**) are what will take your Delivery to the next level. The skills and techniques mentioned in these chapters will show you how to captivate any audience from your first word to your very last.

The following 3 pillars (**Structure**, **Clarity**, and **Impact**) will specifically focus on your Content, giving you a unique edge, so that when you deliver a message, it is remembered and most importantly, acted on every time.

If I was to make one promise, assuming you take regular action on the information presented, you will absolutely feel more confident and inspired to excel in public speaking by the time you reach the last word of this book.

Let's get started!

Chapter 1

BODY LANGUAGE

E"*ffective communication is 20% what you know and 80% what you feel" – Jim Rohn.*

This quote captures the essence of why Body Language is extremely important.

You see 150,000 years ago, when our ancestors were fighting saber-toothed tigers, foraging for food and frantically trying to start fires, spoken language did not exist. Instead, the only form of communication was Body Language. That is why we naturally and subconsciously, read far more into Body Language than the spoken word.

When you stand in front of an audience, they are judging you - often before you have even said your first words. And you will have done this too! For example, have you ever had a sense that a speaker is incredibly nervous before they even start? Or (and this can happen too) that a speaker believes they are too good for the room, before they even begin? Your brain is automatically making these subconscious judgements which eventually form your opinion. Therefore, as Jim Rohn states, *"80% of effective communication is what you feel"*; in other words, it's what you see…

Ultimately, as speakers, we want our audience to form a positive opinion of us – because people buy into people. If I don't like you, I'm less likely to listen to you. Thus, we must consider how we can use Body Language to achieve a positive impression. Before we dive into the key skills to accomplishing this, first, let's establish a clear understanding of what the term 'Body Language' encompasses.

Body Language Fundamentals

Current definitions state that Body Language involves 'conscious and unconscious movements and postures by which attitudes and feelings are communicated'. Taking the key words of 'movements' and 'postures', we can divide Body Language into four key factors:

- **Stance**
- **Gestures**
- **Facial Expression**
- **Eye Contact**

Each of these factors plays a pivotal role in how you communicate. If you have ever seen a nervous speaker, you will most likely notice that their Expression is tense, their Eye Contact is fleeting, their Stance is narrow and unsupportive, and that they rarely use Gestures to emphasise their points. Therefore, how you utilise these four factors is extremely important.

Stance

Imagine you are in the process of building your dream house; you are doing it completely from scratch on a plot of land you have specifically selected. What would be the first step to building this house? Would you start by creating the living room? Would you build the roof? The floor?

If you want your structure to last, you go deeper – by setting up your foundations. In Body Language, your foundation is your <u>Stance.</u> Everything is built up from how you hold your body and position your feet.

The goal is to project confidence; therefore, you need to ensure that your Stance reflects that. This can be achieved through taking the following three positional actions:

➢ **Feet –** Ensure that both feet are firmly planted on the ground, ideally shoulder width apart or slightly further apart. This will give you a solid base, creating stability and will centre you before your presentation begins.

➢ **Body –** Roll your shoulders back to create a straight, upright spine and lift your chest to a comfortable position. Apart from when gesturing, always keep your hands by your side. This body position will make you appear more open and confident to your audience.

> ➢ **Head** - Throughout your presentation keep your head level, ensuring it does not drop too far down as you will have difficultly holding eye contact, or rises too far up as this could be perceived as arrogance. Maintaining a level position should feel natural and will allow you to address the room with ease.

Once you become comfortable with taking this Stance, you can begin to incorporate movement to make your presentation more dynamic and engaging. By movement, I'm referring to how you move around your speaking area.

There are two key benefits to moving instead of staying rooted to the ground:

1. By moving around the stage, you physically become closer to different parts of the audience. This is beneficial because people are more likely to listen if the speaker is standing close to them.

2. Movement can be used as an excellent tool for illustrating different points. Imagine you are doing a speech related to your business/job and you have three key points; what you have done (past), what you are doing (present), and what you will do (future). During your speech, you could use the stage as a timeline; making your first point (past) on the right-hand side, then moving to the middle to talk about the present, before delivering your third point (future) on the left-hand side of the stage. This form of strategic movement makes the structure of

your presentation clear to your audience and creates distinction between your three different points.

However, caution is required! You do not want to use movement without purpose or in a continuous manner (e.g. moving all the time). Instead use movement sparingly to illustrate a change of idea/point or to enhance visual imagery of a story. Keep yourself on track by asking: 'Does this movement add value to my presentation?'. If the answer is no, drop the movement and take a firm stance.

What Not to Do

This may seem self-explanatory, but you would be surprised by some of the odd Stances people take when they feel the pressure of public speaking. Here is a list of points on how NOT to stand - consider if you are guilty of any of these:

- ➤ **The Rocking Boat** – Instead of taking a solid, grounded Stance, this speaker rocks back and forth on their feet, making their audience feel seasick.

- ➤ **The Leaning Tower of Pisa** – This is a balancing act, where the speaker places all of their weight on one foot, while lightly pointing the toe of their other foot towards the ground. Eventually, gravity does its job, and the speaker becomes at risk of falling down.

- ➤ **The Closed Shop** – This speaker has a very closed off body position; making themselves as small as possible by having a slumped posture, their hands clasped across their mid-section and their head tucked down. They appear extremely nervous to an audience.

➢ **The Macho Man –** This is the individual who enjoys the attention of public speaking for all the wrong reasons. Their foot position is uncomfortably wide, testing the fabric of their jeans. Their chest is puffed up like Mr Olympia and they appear to look down on their audience from an elevated head position. You will not make friends by being the macho man.

Remember that your Stance is your foundation. If you can start a speech with good foot, body, and head positioning, this will set you up for success. You will feel stable, in control and confident that you can execute.

Gestures

Gestures are one of the most overlooked tools in public speaking. Their impact can be highly significant in clarifying points and increasing engagement.

Most people Gesture when they are having a conversation one-to-one, but that same majority tend <u>not to Gesture</u> when speaking in public. Once again, the pressure of the situation prevents people from truly showcasing their personality. You can break through that pressure by strategically implementing Gestures which will make you appear more open and approachable and will enhance your verbal message. At first, it may feel unnatural but over time Gestures will become one of the catalysts for your public speaking confidence.

There are two types of Gestures which I would recommend implementing when speaking in public: Open-Palm Gestures and Descriptive Gestures:

Open-Palm

In 2014, Dananjaya Hettiarachchi, a business owner from Sri Lanka, stepped on stage in front of thousands of people and delivered a presentation which would change his life forever. He enthralled his audience with scintillating stories from his past, full of highs and lows with lots of messages to take home. He had the audience laughing, crying and feeling every single part of his journey. Above all, he appeared to have a connection with everyone in the room which was unprecedented. It was clear when he stepped off stage that there could only be one 'World Champion of Public Speaking' that year.

There were many great elements to Dananjaya's World Championship winning speech, but one element which was prominent throughout his speech was his Open-Palm Gestures.

An Open-Palm Gesture is simply when you address the audience while showing the palms of your hands. The importance of this Gesture can be linked back to evolution. In order to preserve survival, your brain has become programmed to focus on the hands of people within close proximity to you - without you even realising. This is because historically, during physical altercations, people have used their hands to punch, scratch and carry weapons which can pose a significant threat to life.

Your brain's job is to keep you alive. Therefore, by reading the hands your brain takes a necessary precaution to ensure your safety. However, this sense of threat can be disbanded by displaying open-palm gestures. Throughout history the Open-Palm Gesture has been synonymous with feelings of trust, honesty, and alliance. Don't believe me? When taking an oath in court people will show the palm of one hand to suggest honesty and integrity, when surrendering, individuals will put both hands in the air to show that they are unarmed and mean no harm, and when wrongly accused, people will naturally hold both palms up and say something like - 'I didn't eat the Jaffa cakes!'.

The Open-Palm is ingrained in our culture, and like Dananjaya, you too can take advantage of that by including more Open-Palm Gestures in your presentations.

Here is an example:

How would you like to be able to display confidence, trust, and openness in the first 2 seconds of your speech? You can achieve that, by starting your presentation with wide open arms (like a hug) and Open-Palms facing the audience. Many people call this Gesture 'the audience hug' as you are welcoming the audience to come with you on a safe journey in which they will be entertained, educated, and inspired.

Going further into the mechanics, this Gesture is effective because it instantly displays confidence when you take up space with your open arms, honesty as your body is completely exposed - in a good way - and promotes trust because you are seen as unarmed. Therefore, you are subconsciously seen as a friend instead of a threat.

In short, the more you use Open-Palm gestures the stronger your rapport will be with your audience.

Descriptive Gestures

Did you know that 65% of the population can be classified as visual learners (Inc., 2017)? In other words, these people learn through visual demonstration. When speaking in public, it is imperative to consider how your audience takes on board information. Too often, presentations are delivered with word-heavy slides, industry-specific examples and a general lack of creativity. You **need** to provide visual demonstrations if you want your information to be remembered by your audience. How can you do that?

Start with Descriptive Gestures.

Descriptive Gestures include any form of hand movement which is specific to a piece of verbal dialogue. For instance, if I was describing to you how I stumbled across the most beautiful alpine lake, I could Gesture downwards (showing you where the lake is on the stage) while articulating how it was a mesmerising mix of emerald greens, blues & turquoises. When detailing the nearby mountains beyond the lake I could Gesture upwards –

recounting how they were tall, defined and had white tips at the very top. Lastly, I could Gesture to my left when describing the location of the close-by wooden gamekeeper's hut, which sat at the edge of this gorgeous lake. The goal is to use these forms of gestures to help convey vivid imagery for your audience.

Descriptive Gestures are not just confined to describing locations. They can also be used to describe people, emotions, and objects. You may describe a large, strong individual by moving your arms from your side slightly out and tensing to indicate size. You might Gesture quickly and frequently to suggest a feeling of excitement or you might slump your arms and move slower to convey defeat. If describing the solar system, you may use a joined circle hand motion to describe the sun in the middle, before pointing out the different planets which orbit.

Remember, the purpose of Gesturing is to enhance your verbal message; therefore, your Gestures (specifically descriptive) must be in sync with your words in order to build strong, beneficial imagery. If performed correctly, such Gestures will improve the learning experience of your audience and will make your presentations far more engaging.

Facial Expression

To fully understand the power of Facial Expression I would like to invite you into the world of comedy. Arguably no other field uses Facial Expressions more effectively to convey emotions than comedians/comical actors.

A prime example is Rowan Atkinson. His portrayal of the character Mr. Bean is legendary for having audiences in stitches while they watch this childish man try to complete the most mundane of daily tasks. Interestingly, most of the humour in the show does not actually occur due to dialogue, but rather due to the Facial Expressions Atkinson portrays. This is a theme which is often seen in stand-up comedy performance as well. Yes, the words of the joke are funny, but the commitment of the <u>Facial Expression</u> takes it to another level.

However, Facial Expressions are not just restricted to having an impact in comedy, they can be used to convey a full range of emotions within presentations. Excitement can be conveyed by smiling more often, passion can be portrayed by being dynamic with your expression, a sense of seriousness comes across when you move your face less and narrow your brow and finally sadness can be seen when the corners of your mouth point down while your eyebrows rise up.

But you know this already, because you see it every single day when you interact with another person. Most people, some more than others, wear their emotions through their expression, and research has shown that we are extremely proficient at interpreting what different Facial Expressions mean (Ekman, 1992).

Herein lies the problem: people often do not express themselves when speaking in public. How many speakers have you seen who present with a blank face? Who look disinterested? Who give the impression that they just do not want to be there? They might not want to be there, and I understand that, but by presenting in such a tedious manner, they are not only boring their audience to death but also, they are wasting their own time.

If you do not want to waste your time and would like to keep your audience engaged, make sure you incorporate Facial Expressions within your presentation. An easy one to start with, which will help you build rapport and also calm your nerves, is to smile. Smiling during your presentation is fantastic for a number of reasons:

1. When you smile, people smile back. Seeing people smile back at you will encourage you to keep going as you will see that the audience is on your side.

2. You appear more approachable when you smile. Remember one of the goals of your presentation should be that people approach you afterwards for business development purposes/to ask questions. This is far more likely to happen if you smile.

3. You give the impression that you actually want to be there! Remember that problem we spoke about before - speakers having blank faces? A smile will change all of that because it shows that you are passionate, that you have valuable information to share and that you are worth listening to.

Use the power of Facial Expression in your presentations. Remember its less about the words you say and more about how you make the audience feel.

Eye Contact

Have you ever been in a situation where you are having a conversation with a work colleague, but they are not looking you in the eye?

How did this make you feel? Were you frustrated? Concerned? Did you feel like they were not listening to you? Would you trust them?

We have all felt through experience the importance of holding Eye Contact during a conversation, yet we fail to do it during our presentations!

Most speakers look at their notes, they look at their PowerPoint slideshow and the last place they tend to look is in their audiences' eyes; even though their audience is who they are trying to connect with. It is extremely difficult to build rapport with an audience if you spend the whole time looking at a piece of paper. They will feel exactly how you felt when that work colleague did not look at you...

The Nightmare

However, I do understand completely why speakers are reluctant to let go of their notes and fully embrace their audience. It's because of 'The Nightmare'.

The shared nightmare everyone has, regardless of their speaking experience, goes something like this:

You walk towards the front of the room, feeling the anticipation building, your heart beating, and your mind racing before you go to battle. You make it to the podium and turn around to see hundreds of piercing, staring, judging eyes, looking at YOU...

Suddenly, you feel the full enormity of the situation; everyone is waiting, expecting you to deliver. You go to say your first words, the words you've practised for weeks, the words you know off by heart, the words you've dreamed about...

But these words don't come out...

Your memory has betrayed you, as you stand there completely exposed, wishing the ground would swallow you whole...

Obviously, we do not want that to happen. Unless you are very experienced and are at the stage where you are comfortable with facing that possibility, I would never ask you to speak without notes or a PowerPoint.

However, what I would ask is that you adopt the **90/10 rule**. 90% of the time you should be looking and interacting with your audience – engaging with them fully. The other 10% can be used to 'glance' (emphasis on 'glance') at your notes.

In order to make sure you only 'glance' and not 'read' from your notes, I would recommend condensing your notes into short 'triggering' bullet points. These should be no longer than 10 words (the shorter the better) and should provide a 'trigger' for your memory which gets you back on track.

For example, if I was doing a presentation on the benefits of investing in property, three of my bullet points could be:

- Passive Income
- Location Value
- Clear Exit Strategy

Therefore, when I glance and see 'passive income' that will trigger my memory and remind me to talk about a range of different points around that topic; holiday lets, tenants, hours required could be some examples.

Thus, the 90/10 rule frees up your mind and calms your nerves; because you have that reassurance that your notes are nearby which, in turn, allows you to make good quality eye contact with your audience.

Too Much

Now that we have found a quality compromise to looking at notes, there is one other possibility we must consider when looking at our audience – making too much Eye Contact.

This is often seen in speakers who are overly confident and who try to bully their audience through intimidation until they see their point of view. Assertiveness certainly does have its place in public speaking. However, you can be assertive without being involved in a forced staring contest with a terrified audience member.

The Sweet Spot

We do not want too much Eye Contact and we certainly do not want too little; therefore, we need to find middle ground.

In my experience, the optimum amount of time to hold Eye Contact with an audience member is 2-3 seconds. This is enough time to make the audience member feel addressed, but not too long so that they feel uncomfortable.

Once you have completed 2-3 seconds with one person, move onto another audience member, and then another one, so that you are covering the entire room from front to back. If you have a large audience in front of you, do not worry; simply pick out one person in the room and hold the same length of Eye Contact as before. The beauty with large crowds is that if you look at one person, everyone around that individual will feel as if you are looking at them too. Thus, you can cover the room without looking at every single attendee.

This may all sound simple and straightforward but please do not overlook the power of Eye Contact. In public speaking, trust is an absolute must and effective Eye Contact will help you achieve that.

SEO

Obviously, remembering all of the above details about your Stance, Gestures, Facial Expression and Eye Contact would be quite challenging when you're about to start speaking and you are feeling the pressure.

So, to simplify, I want you to initially focus on **SEO.** No, that does not stand for Search Engine Optimisation, but rather it stands for; **S**mile, **E**ye Contact & **O**pen. We've covered these three points above in depth:

- ✓ <u>Smiling</u> will help you come across as enthusiastic and approachable
- ✓ <u>Eye contact</u> held effectively will promote trust and connection
- ✓ <u>Open Body Language</u> will make you appear confident

These three points incorporate perfectly, the 4 key factors of Body Language which we explored at the beginning of this chapter:

- <u>Stance</u> and <u>Gestures</u> through 'Open Body Language'.
- <u>Facial Expression</u> by 'Smiling'
- <u>Eye Contact</u> speaks for itself.

Of course, once you become more experienced you can begin to focus more on the finer details of each factor. But when starting, concentrate on nailing the basics through **SEO.**

Your Action Point

In your '15-minutes of action' practice implementing **SEO.**....

A good way to immediately practice this, during your 15-minutes, is to pretend you are starting an upcoming presentation. Focus on nailing the opening two minutes of that speech by ensuring that you <u>Smile</u>, have good <u>Eye Contact</u>, and your Body Language remains <u>Open</u> throughout. You might find it useful to video yourself when doing this task – that way you can watch it back and see for yourself how you are coming across. I think you will be surprised by the difference SEO makes!

When implementing **SEO,** you will face two key challenges:

1. You will make mistakes
2. It will seem unnatural

Here is how to deal with both obstacles:

1. **Break it down** – instead of trying to achieve everything in your first attempt, focus on one at a time. For instance, at first you may just concentrate on Smiling more during your presentations. Once this feels more natural, try improving your Eye Contact. In time, move onto creating 'Open' Body Language. By taking a step-by-step approach, you break down the challenge into manageable chunks which will give you a better chance of success.

2. **Fake it until you become it** – Yes, at first **SEO** will seem incredibly unnatural. You may even question whether you are being authentic or not. However, if your intention is to become a more confident, engaging speaker who puts their audiences first… do not worry. You are simply on the journey to achieving that long-term goal. Your first time won't be your best time. But with time, practice and patience, **SEO** will complement your already unique speaking style, and you will become the speaker you want to be.

Share on Social Media

Share your progress online by using the social media hashtag: - **#5PillarsPublicSpeaking.** If used on LinkedIn, I will comment on your post and answer any questions you may have on Body Language.

Chapter 2

VOICE

Recently I had the opportunity to look back at a short presentation I delivered when I was just 17 years old.

As I stated before, I was not naturally a good public speaker and this footage is testament to that. My Body Language was closed, Gestures and Eye Contact were at a minimum, and I seemed to almost be 'hiding' behind the podium I was speaking from. But what stood out most of all was how boring my Voice was…

I spoke using the same monotonous pace, volume, and tone throughout. I can confidently say on that day I undoubtedly put the entire room to sleep!

Comparing my speaking style from then to now, I believe the most significant difference is how I use my Voice. My Voice is one of my biggest strengths and that is because I utilise its full range to evoke emotions, create imagery and entertain.

People wonder; what makes a speaker charismatic? What makes a speaker special? How can they have an entire audience hanging onto their every word?

The answer is how they use their **Voice.** In this chapter, you will discover how you can transform your voice to become compelling, respected, and persuasive. But before we get into these details, first we must consider the opposite.

The Monotone Speaker

Listening to a Monotone Speaker is like watching grass grow - not very exciting. Much like a Harry Potter Dementor, these individuals suck the life out of their audience. They create unbelievable boredom which prevents any form of positive impression being made. This is because, like in my teenage speech, the speaker fails to vary their Voice in any way, shape or form.

Think of speaking like driving a car. Imagine you are driving along a motorway; you are going at a moderate speed, there are very few cars around and the road is completely straight. Maybe Kenny Rogers is playing on the radio and overall, there is very little for you to think about.

Would you agree that in a situation like this, it is quite easy for miles and miles to pass by without you even realising?

Of course, it is – because there is no variation. It's the same with speaking - if you have a Monotone Voice, your speech will pass by your audience without them even realising.

Therefore, the key to avoid the curse of the Monotone Speaker is to get off the monotone motorway! You need to include variation in your voice. Keeping it simple; there are three fundamental ways in which you **must** vary your voice:

> ➢ **Tonality**
> ➢ **Tempo**
> ➢ **Volume**

These three methods can be remembered by the acronym **TTV**. For the rest of this chapter, we will explore these methods and will determine how you can implement each in your future presentations.

Tonality

Tonality can be described as the way your voice sounds when you say something. You see, in conversation we tend to focus less on the words and concentrate more on how they are said.

Imagine you are meeting up with a friend for a coffee. When you arrive, you may ask,

 "So, how are you?" and they might reply *"I'm feeling great"*.

Now depending on how they say these three words, you can interpret that response in many different ways. If said in a quiet voice with low energy and little conviction, you will innately know that something is off and that they do not actually *'feel great'*. However, if your friend says,

 'I'm feeling great' in an upbeat, high-energy voice like Tony the Tiger from the Frosties cereal, you then know that friend is absolutely fine.

Our ears are attuned to picking up even the slightest of differences in Tonality – a point worth considering when speaking in public. Ultimately, our goal is to use Tonality to evoke different emotions in our audience.

Going back to our driving analogy – think of Tonality like the twists and turns of a road. Suddenly you have to pay a lot closer attention to your commute compared to being on that straight 'monotone motorway'.

After a lot of trial and error, I have found that there are four key Tonalites which work exceptionally well in business presentations. These four **Tonalites** are:

- **Mystery**
- **Understanding**
- **Excitement**
- **Certainty**

Mystery

The Tone of Mystery is used to evoke one specific human emotion – curiosity. It makes your audience wonder what is coming next.

A speaker who uses the Tone of Mystery to fantastic effect is astrophysicist, Neil deGrasse Tyson. There is a stereotype that physicists and academic professors, while deeply knowledgeable in their chosen field, are in general very boring to listen to. Neil deGrasse Tyson is the outlier in this trend. He uses the full capabilities of his voice to draw you in, evoke curiosity and have you on the edge of your seat. Unquestionably, he is a master at creating anticipation in his presentations.

But how can you implement the Tone of Mystery? Here are some simple steps to follow:

1. **Lower your voice** – draw your audience in by making them listen closely.

2. **Tease your audience -** have a smoothness and confidence to your voice which suggests you know the answer, but you are not sure if they do.

3. **Breathe on your words** - when delivering key words in your sentence, exhale to create a breathy voice - a sense of wonder will feel palpable around the room.

It is important to consider when you should use this Tonality. Use it too often and it will lose its potency; use it in the wrong place and you will come across as, well, strange! Thus, when is the best time?

Arguably, the best time is when you are posing a question. Because a question naturally encourages audience members to think; adding mystery to that question will build anticipation for what the answer will be. In a sense, it brings the question to life! Obviously, a great place to insert a question, rhetorical or not, is at the start of your speech. If you can stir that curiosity at the start, the feeling will continue throughout.

Understanding

Former United States President Bill Clinton has a very chequered past. Nevertheless, in 1992, Bill Clinton did something which was absolutely extraordinary. So extraordinary, that it won the hearts of an entire nation, crushed his competition, and arguably secured his 1992 Presidential Election success.

This miraculous feat took place in Richmond, Virginia, during a Town Hall debate where incumbent Republican President George H.W. Bush Snr. was up against the young, hungry Bill Clinton of the Democrats.

Things got interesting when a local woman stood up near the front, and asked both Presidential candidates a very direct, punchy question. She asked,

"How has the national debt personally affected each of your lives? And if it hasn't, how can you honestly find a cure for the economic problems of the common people if you have no experience in what's ailing them?"

George Bush Snr. went first; initially questioning the purpose of the question, before avoiding answering how debt had affected him personally, and then deflecting the question by stating he had 'met' people who had been personally affected.

Then it was Bill's turn. He immediately stood up and approached the woman while asking, *"You know people who have lost their jobs and homes?"*. She nodded in agreement. Bill then went on to give a direct answer on how he had been personally affected by debt, through government cuts forcing him to do more with less. He spoke about how he had met people all around the country who were just like this woman; struggling, suffering and with little support around them.

He ended by giving a solution to this crisis, *"I believe we must invest in American jobs, American education and bring the American people together again..."*.

After that it was abundantly clear that only one man was winning this election, and it wasn't George Bush Snr. Although the structure of Bill Clinton's response was impressive, what truly had an impact on that woman, the audience, and the millions watching at home was how he spoke to her. He spoke to her in such a way that made her feel heard, understood, and respected. He spoke to her with **Understanding**.

Used correctly, the Tone of Understanding is phenomenal at building strong rapport, trust, and connection with your audience. It illustrates to audience members that you understand them, that you want to help them and that you are just like them.

How can you implement it? Here are three simple steps to follow:

1. **Soften your voice** – in order to be successful, you need to convey compassion and understanding and softening your tone can help portray that.

2. **Speak to one person** – you need to make a connection, and in order to do that you must speak as if you are completely focusing your attention on one person. This is not a performance; it is a one-to-one conversation in front of many people.

3. **Like a friend** – Lastly, speak to the audience like you would speak to a friend who is going through a challenging time. You would be sensitive when discussing why they are upset, but strong when suggesting a solution moving forward.

If you are describing an audience's or client's challenges and problems, use this Tonality to demonstrate that you understand what they are going through. This will help you build outstanding rapport as your audience will feel heard, understood, and respected.

On a side note, the tone of Understanding is extremely powerful, can convince people to form alliances and does create a deep sense of trust. Therefore, please only use this with good intentions in mind.

Excitement

The word excite, comes from the Latin verb 'excitare' which means to 'rouse, call out or summon forth'. It is entirely down to you as a speaker to 'summon forth' excitement from your audience. And one of the best ways in which you can do this is using the Tone of **Excitement**.

Have you ever been watching a speaker and thought, "*Wow, he or she loves what they do!*"? It's infectious and creates an amazing energy in the room which everyone takes on board.

A superb example of a speaker who lives and breathes passion and enthusiasm is motivational speaker, TV host and author, Mel Robbins. Her highly popular TEDx talk – '*How to Stop Screwing Yourself Over*' is a great example of her compelling speaking style. She brings tremendous energy to the room, making the audience laugh, smile and in one case, became physically involved when she unexpectedly prodded a man who was wearing a Hawaiian shirt! She breaks the TEDx rules by jumping from the stage into the audience and at one point, even showed pictures of naked Barbie dolls. Although the prodding, jumping and Barbie images are to generate some excitement, what really lifts the energy is her Voice. Here is how you can do the same:

1. **Speed** – Excitement does not move slowly. You need pace, momentum, and directness to grab attention and lift the energy of the room. The audience, within reason, needs to keep up with you!

2. **Upbeat** – Your voice needs to radiate positivity, so make sure your tone is cheerful and friendly, as though you are almost encouraging your audience to join in.

3. **Loose** - To create a sense of fun you cannot be rigid with your voice. So be dynamic, play outside the box, and create that excitement through the freedom you grant your voice.

I believe the vast majority of presentations need to include the Tone of Excitement. Too many times audiences are bored senseless because passion and excitement are absent. How can you expect someone to care about what you say if the topic does not even excite *you*?

Flip the script, be bold, and use the Tone of **Excitement** to energise your audience.

Certainty

It's the 28th August 1963: 250,000 civil rights activists are converging towards the Lincoln Memorial in Washington D.C. They move with purpose, passion, and the belief that they can make a difference; partly because they know what they are campaigning for is morally right, and partly because of the man who is leading them.

That afternoon, Martin Luther King Jnr. made his way to the podium and delivered a speech which would change the lives of millions, would change the course of history, and would have a profound impact on generations to come.

This speech included four key words which would be remembered for the rest of time, '*I have a dream*'.

I want you to think about that famous speech; hear the words, visualise the black and white footage; for a moment, pretend you are there in the crowd. Now let me ask you this; when you heard Martin Luther King deliver that speech in his strong, powerful voice, did you doubt him? Did you question his words? Did you think, "*Hmm not sure this guy knows what he's talking about*"?

Of course not. Not only because he is morally correct, but also because of how he delivered his words. They were delivered with intensity, passion and a real conviction which simply could not be disputed. He inspired the world to change with his **Certainty.**

You see, people make decisions based on how 'confident' they feel. Imagine you have got into some trouble with the law. You have been summoned to court; the verdict of your case is in the balance - what do you do?

You hire a lawyer. Now, your decision on who you hire will be based, of course, on cost and availability, but more significantly, it will be based on your level of confidence. You are not going to hire someone who you believe does not have the capability to win your case. You will hire the individual who gives you the greatest sense of confidence that they can deliver the result you are looking for.

Why is this so important? When you are presenting in public, often you are trying to convince your audience to do something. There is always a goal. Whatever it is, the success of that persuasion will be determined by the confidence your audience has in you, your product, your service or your new way of thinking. Unless forced by fear, people will not take on board your ideas if they do not believe in them. Therefore, to achieve our presentation goals, we need to make our audience feel <u>certain</u> that our ideas will work. Here are some tips on how to achieve this:

1. **Strong** – In these moments you must have a strong voice which does not waver or break. Achieve this by breathing more deeply, taking your time, and speak as though you are profoundly serious about your subject.

2. **Emphasise** – During various stages of your presentation, emphasise key words and points that you want to resonate with your audience. You can achieve this by lingering on these words for longer and heightening your volume when you hit them.

3. **Passion** - Speak with intensity and emotion by allowing yourself to express your true feelings. This comes out naturally in conversation so give yourself permission to use it on stage.

The **Tone** of **Certainty** is an immensely powerful tool which can influence people to make decisions they may not have otherwise considered. Be responsible when using this Tonality, as your credibility will plummet if you cannot deliver on your promises. That said, the best time to use it is when you are making a key point or encouraging people to take action. For instance, if your Call to Action is at the end of your presentation, finish with **Certainty**.

Tonality Summary

There you have it – four powerful Tonalities which can evoke the emotions of *Mystery*, *Understanding*, *Excitement* and *Certainty* within your audience.

The key is to try and implement each one within your presentation as they can complement each other. Start your presentation by creating curiosity to grab attention, before transitioning into an anecdote which strategically builds rapport with your audience. Later you may want to lift the energy in the room and at the end you might choose to hit home your key message. One Tonality can lead into the next, which takes your audience on an emotional journey towards your Key Message.

Tempo

Returning to our car on the highway analogy, Tonality has helped us introduce some twists and turns on our road making our commute a lot more interesting. However, there are other elements that can be improved which will take us even further away from the 'monotone motorway'. How about we change the speed at which we are driving?

When presenting, changing the speed at which you speak can have an extraordinary impact on your audience's level of engagement.

While I was studying at university, I went along to an entrepreneurial event which was expected to inspire students to become business owners, needle movers and highly driven individuals. It sounded great, but in reality, the event was extremely boring - not because of the topic, but because of the speakers. They spoke at the same monotone pace throughout, turning an extremely exciting, dynamic subject into the dullest experience on the planet. There were casualties in the audience that day! However, this all changed when the last speaker took to the stage.

He had a boldness about him, an air of confidence, and when he spoke, he used something which I had never seen in university before - speed. Not the drug, but rather the pace at which he was speaking. It was relentless, captivating and lifted the energy of the entire room. An audience that had been sentenced to death by the other speakers, was all of a sudden alive, interacting, laughing and absolutely buzzing. This man's energy was infectious and left us hanging from the ceiling.

Ultimately, the speaker achieved that incredible reaction by doing a number of things exceptionally well - but the standout technique was his speed.

When you speak to an audience at a high speed and in a confident manner, they are highly likely to stay engaged for several reasons:

- **Shock** – most speakers deliver their presentations in a terribly slow monotonous way, so speaking at speed can be quite shocking. It catches your audience off-guard, makes you stand out and creates a sense of urgency.

- **Momentum** – put simply, speaking fast builds strong energy in the room. I guarantee that if you speak fast and make your presentation interactive, (which you should) your audience's responses will come at a fast pace too. They will not waste time looking at their phones or talking about nonsense. Instead, they will get straight to work on the activity you have set because they are following your lead.

- **FOMO** – speaking fast can quite literally create FOMO (Fear Of Missing Out) for your audience. This is because they are afraid that if they lose focus, they will miss a key part of your presentation as you are moving so fast. Therefore, by speaking at pace you are not giving your audience an opportunity to switch off. However, as we will now discuss, this is a balancing act.

The Danger of Speed

Although speaking fast can lift the energy of the room and increase audience engagement, this is only true if the speed is accompanied by confidence. We've all seen it; a speaker comes to the stage, who is clearly nervous and begins to talk as fast as humanly possible to get the presentation over and done with as quickly as they can.

If you speak too fast for too long you will exhaust your audience and they will literally 'give up' on trying to keep up with your presentation. Furthermore, pace delivered without control sends a message to the audience that the speaker is not fully confident in their ideas, as competence is usually accompanied by composure.

So, what is the solution? How do you keep the energy high without exhausting the audience or coming across as anxious?

The answer - Variation.

By all means, during parts of your presentation speak with pace, intensity and passion. But remember to supplement that high energy with pauses, patience and emphasis. In short, speak at a slower pace too.

Slowing Down & The Pause

As mentioned before, it is detrimental to speak at a slow, lethargic pace throughout your entire presentation. However, slowing down for short periods of time can be an extremely powerful method for conveying ideas and emotions. Let's talk about the famous 'Pause'.

I remember the first time I successfully used a Pause during a high-stakes presentation. It was in front of 600 business school students. This was my first large scale professional presentation.

I was still a student myself and little green. One of the lecturers at the university introduced me. He referred to me as, *'The Public Speaking Guru'* (I've always hated the word *'guru'*) and went on to say, *"that I was going to share wisdom and knowledge which would blow them all away"*. The audience collectively and understandably rolled their eyes. A great start...

For a moment I stared out at the hundreds of unimpressed, uninterested, young faces staring back at me. I started to feel the pressure of the situation and stumbled into my opening lines,

"Hi, hope you are all well today and are ready to energise your lives with public speaking".

Cringe! With that great start the audience looked extremely unconvinced. I tentatively went on to explain that we were going to cover different aspects of public speaking; planning, preparation, delivery and overcoming 'the fear' – the feeling of indifference was now palpable in the room.

But then I did something which changed this dynamic.

I changed gears and began speaking to the audience directly. I spoke about how they should see public speaking as an important tool which can be used in job interviews, work presentations, university projects and business pitches. I made it abundantly clear that if they wanted to start a business or be in the top 10% of their future organisation, they **needed** to embrace public speaking....

…………… (Pause)

Just like now, I left a prolonged Pause, and I swear that day you would have been able to hear a pin drop. It felt really good!

Pausing is effective for several reasons:

1. **Attention Grabbing** – it deviates from the norm. Audiences expect speakers to be talking continuously and therefore, breaks of silence stand out in their minds.

2. **Allows time to think –** the period of silence gives audience members an opportunity to digest the information you have just shared.

Consequently, it allows your message/point to resonate more deeply in the minds of your audience.

3. **Confidence** – there is no skill in public speaking that displays confidence more than a deliberate, well-placed Pause. To have the composure to make your audience wait, showcases that you are fully in control and have tremendous belief in your abilities.

When it comes to specifically using the Pause, I would recommend implementing this technique after you make a significant statement or when asking a rhetorical question. You can identify whether a statement is significant or not by asking yourself, *'How important is this statement to my presentation?'*. If the 'importance' is low, there is no need for a Pause. If the importance is high (i.e. you want the audience never to forget this point), then include a Pause.

Aside from using the 'Pause', another occasion where slowing down can be extremely effective is when you are conveying negative emotions. Remember speed is associated with positive emotions (enthusiasm, excitement etc), therefore slowing down is closely related to negative emotions.

This will be covered in more detail in the next chapter, but for now it is important to note that, at times, it can be very endearing to 'open up' to your audience. If you can share challenges and difficulties you have faced, you will build strong rapport with the room, because audience members will be able relate to your story. Ultimately, we have all, at some point, been through hard times.

Combining Fast with Slow

Before we move onto the last part of **Voice**, I want to share with you a proven technique that combines the positive elements of both speaking fast and slowing down. I call this 'The Sudden Stop'.

Let's say you have an important point in your presentation, and you want to maintain the energy in the room before delivering that point. What you can do initially is start that chain of dialogue by speaking very quickly, lifting the energy of the room, and engaging the entire crowd; once you feel they are all paying attention and are excited to be there – i.e. the energy is at an all-time high - deliver your message and, Stop…

By performing the 'Sudden Stop' you benefit from the best of both worlds; the speed of delivery lifts the energy and maintains engagement and the Pause (or stop) ensures that the key message is heard. You can perform this technique multiple times in your presentation to great effect.

Volume

On our car journey we now have twists and turns in the road (**Tonality**) and also changes of speed (**Tempo**). The last ingredient we need to include to make this the most engaging car journey of your life is to change the landscape of the road. Driving through a mountain tunnel with the engine sound echoing off the tunnel walls feels and sounds vastly different to cruising through an open, peaceful valley. Likewise, changing the level of your **Volume** creates a noticeable difference in the experience for your audience.

Of the three techniques, I would suggest that Volume is the easiest to implement and will yield the fastest results.

This is because there are only two options; increase or decrease.

Imagine a long, blue horizontal line stretched across the middle of a piece of white paper. This flat, straight line represents your standard speaking Volume. It should not be too high (as you could cause discomfort) or too low (as you could risk not being heard). It requires to be right in the middle where you can be heard clearly, and it is pleasant for your audience to listen to.

Although we want to stay on this straight line for most of the time, we do not want to restrict ourselves. Remember, with no variation comes no engagement. Eventually, your audience will naturally switch off once they become accustomed to the rhythm of your voice. To avoid this, we must occasionally break the pattern of the straight line. This can be achieved by including small **Spikes** and **Dips** of Volume within your speaking dialogue.

Spikes

Spikes of volume are a fantastic method for literally grabbing your audience's attention. If you feel you are losing the attention of people in the room, this should be your 'go-to' move to bring them back. Display this technique by sharply increasing the volume of your voice for a short period of time before dropping back down to your straight line. The reason you only lift the Volume for a short period is because if you hold it constantly for long periods (e.g. one minute plus) you will be shouting at your audience – and no-one likes to be shouted at. It is possible to include Spikes of Volume during any part of your presentation. Spikes can complement words which are strongly emphasised and can also contribute to lifting the energy when increasing speed.

My top tip would be to include a technique which I call '**The Striking Sentence'**.

This is when you increase the Volume of your voice significantly for the first word, or words, at the start of your sentence.

For example, if I were to say using only my straight line, standard voice; - '*Something which is interesting...*' it would not grab your attention. However, if I were deploying The Striking Sentence via placing emphasis on the first word e.g., saying; - '***SOMETHING*** *which is interesting...*' it would be far more engaging.

Which one do you find more engaging? Do you agree it is the second one?

The idea behind **The Striking Sentence** is that the shock increase of volume at the start grabs the attention and then dropping down allows you to maintain that attention throughout the course of your sentence.

Dips

Dips of Volume can be extremely effective for drawing your audience in closer. Do you remember when you were at school, playing in the playground? Everyone was having fun playing tig, swinging on the swings, and running around laughing and screaming. Until, one of your friends whispered something into the ear of the other. All of a sudden you felt left out, confused and compelled to find out what the secret was.

If you lower your voice in a presentation, people will tend to listen more closely as they feel as if they are being 'let in' on a secret. However, only perform Dips for a short period of time (20 seconds or less), because the risk with this technique is that your Volume goes down too low, causing the audience difficulty in hearing you. Dips of Volume cannot be thrown in as sporadically as Spikes, but what you can do is create engrossing transitions.

For example, at the start of a sentence you may begin with a high level of Volume before transitioning down to your baseline. From there, you can continue to gradually lower the Volume of your voice; becoming lower and lower with each word, until you have the entire audience on board, listening intently to your every word.

Your Action Point

Now that you understand how imperative it is to vary your voice through using **Tonality, Tempo and Volume (TTV)**, it is important that you put these principles into practice immediately.

As I mentioned before the easiest, out of the three, to grasp and implement is **Volume**. Your action point is to start including 'Spikes' of Volume in your presentations. During your 15 minutes of action, practice using Spikes at the start of your sentences and record it. Afterwards, play back the recording and notice the difference in the engagement you feel. From there, look to include these Spikes of Volume in front of an actual audience.

After you have achieved that small win, attempt to use dips, followed by variation in **Tempo** and then finally develop your four key **Tonalities**: Mystery, Understanding, Excitement and Certainty.

By taking these small, achievable steps, you will gradually improve your speaking voice at a pace which you can control.

Share on Social Media

Please show me your progress, by posting on LinkedIn with the hashtag - **#5PillarsPublicSpeaking**. If you upload footage of you using the Voice techniques mentioned in this chapter, I will comment with positive and constructive feedback.

Chapter 3

SPEECH STRUCTURE Part 1, The End

So far, we have looked at how we can improve our delivery in public speaking through projecting confident body language and varying our voices to create greater engagement. Now we are going to discuss the other, equally important part of public speaking – **Content**.

As mentioned in the introduction, Content is important because it provides the value for your audience.

In addition, a key element to making your content flow and stand out is how you structure your presentation. A poorly planned structure will lead to poor results. Therefore, it is imperative that we spend time planning and creating our **Speech Structure** to maximise our possibility for success.

In this chapter we will look at how to create a speech from start to finish so that the audience buy into you, your expertise and ultimately, your offering.

As this chapter covers a lot of ground, I have split it into 3 easy to process parts. Each part has its own action point – these activities will help you connect all 3 parts together and will make the content relevant to the presentations you have coming up.

53

Where to Start

In every presentation, there is a beginning, a middle and an end. The question is – where should you start?

The obvious answer is The Beginning. Now although logical, this may not make practical sense.

If you start from the beginning, you run the risk of:

1. **Facing a creative block** – because you are designing your presentation 'off the cuff', line by line, this may lead to you running out of steam.

2. **Failing to achieve your objective** – as you have not defined your End Destination, you may find it more challenging to hit your objective since you do not know where you are going.

Imagine two ships departing from your local harbour; both have the same technology and capable crews. The difference is, one knows exactly where it is going; the Port of San Juan in Peru. Meanwhile, the other ship does not know where it is going, but the crew are going to figure it out on the way. Which ship is more likely to reach its destination?

Obviously the one that knows where it's going. Even although Peru is far away, it still has that end destination in mind. When you are creating a presentation, you need to have your end destination in mind too. Therefore, the best place to start creating a speech is not at The Start, but rather at **The End**.

The End

To establish what your end destination looks like, ask yourself this question,

 "W*hat is the **Purpose** of my presentation?*"

The Purpose may be to sell a product or service; to encourage your team to take a new course of action; to educate people on a specific topic; or to inspire. Truly consider why you are spending time creating and delivering this presentation, as that will reveal your destination.

A Strong Purpose

Ultimately, a strong purpose benefits two key groups: <u>the audience and you.</u>

In every presentation, you always want your Purpose to improve the lives of your audience. You should genuinely want to improve their knowledge and understanding, skillsets, outlook on life and, if applicable, even relieve their pain. If your Purpose does not make a significant difference to one of these outcomes, you are wasting their time and your time.

However, it cannot just be the audience who benefits, otherwise your enthusiasm will dip, and your performance will as well. You need a piece of the pie too. Your slice might come in the form of money, accolades, introductions, or future opportunities. Part of your Purpose needs to be inherently selfish so that you remain inspired to be at your best. Be comfortable with that reality – we all have an ego – it doesn't make you a bad person to accept that.

The true magic happens when there is synergy between the way both the audience benefits and you benefit. In other words, your Purpose satisfies the needs of both groups. Here are some examples:

A Life Coach is speaking to an audience about how to overcome anxiety. His end Purpose is to gain new clients. Now, some audience members may have the goal of overcoming their anxiety. Therefore, the Purpose of this presentation benefits both the audience and the coach; as motivated individuals have the opportunity to learn, while the coach profits financially.

A university lecturer and her students can be equally motivated by exam grades. High scores for the students mean better work opportunities when they graduate. Likewise, good grades mean better promotion opportunities for the lecturer. With these end benefits in mind both groups will be motivated to make the most of their class lectures.

Even those who choose to speak for free and look for nothing in return, adhere to this principle as well. A Motivational Speaker's purpose might be simply to inspire their audience - no strings attached. Fair enough. But a closer examination shows that this specific purpose actually does benefit both groups; the audience become inspired to reach new heights and the speaker's brand and presentation opportunities elevate too – as they are invited to speak at more events.

Consider the Purpose of your future presentation – does it benefit both your audience and you? Find the correct alignment so that both groups feel energised, inspired and satisfied by the end of your presentation.

Call to Action

Once you have a strong, clear Purpose you must now marry that Purpose with an equally powerful Call to Action.

As mentioned in the opening chapter, it is critical to accept that the effectiveness of a presentation can be determined by whether your audience acts on your words or not.

For example, if I am a restauranteur and the purpose of my presentation is to raise funds from investors for a brand new location I am opening, I can gauge my success by whether audience members invest in my new project or not.

Likewise, if I am a sales manager at a call centre and my presentation purpose is to ensure staff can handle objections more effectively on the phone, I can judge the success of my intervention by whether my staff handle objections more successfully or not.

To swing the odds in our favour, we include a Call to Action to prompt our audience to act on our words – in turn, making our presentation a success.

As a rule, always try to include a Call to Action at the end of every professional presentation you give. Remember, when in a professional environment you are not just there to have a laugh or pass the time. Your presentation should be designed to achieve something important – include a **Call to Action** to make it count!

Call to Action Specifics

The most effective *Calls to Action (CTA)* all have three key elements in common, they are:

- ➢ **Positioned** correctly
- ➢ **Achievable**
- ➢ **Time Dependent**

Positioning:

In terms of **Positioning**, insert your **CTA** near the end of your presentation. The reason for this is:

What is said last, **lasts with** your audience.

By using this strategy, you will take advantage of the 'Recency Effect' - the tendency for a person to recall recent information more accurately. By positioning your CTA at the end, audience members will be more likely to remember what you said and what you want them to do.

Achievable:

Alongside, correctly Positioning your CTA, you also want to make sure that your request is Achievable.

Imagine I'm a Personal Trainer working with a new client who has very little training experience. Now, do you think that client would remain motivated to train if I set them the goal of looking like Dwayne 'The Rock' Johnson within the space of a week? No, they might try – but once they see they have made little or no progress within the space of a week, they will stop and give up. The same result will happen with your audience if you make your CTA unachievable. You need to give your audience a next step which they can see themselves attaining.

The key to accomplishing this is to create your CTA based around what your audience can control. The action you are asking them to take must be something which is not influenced by external forces but is instead completely within the individual's hands.

For example, I would make the CTA for my gym client to train 3 times per week. This target is something which is in their hands – they decide if they find the time to train or not.

Time Dependent:

The last ingredient to create a very fruitful Call to Action is for it to be Time Dependent. How many times have you said, *"I'll do it tomorrow,"* and then tomorrow comes and guess what? It still hasn't been done.

Most people procrastinate, in some form, every single day. We put things off, we wait for the 'perfect time' or life gets in the way and we may completely forget about the task altogether. Your audience might have the intention of acting on your words, but as time passes that motivation is likely to dip – causing zero action to be taken.

It is important to understand, as speakers, we cannot completely control what our audience does after our presentation. However, we can give our audience the best chance of succeeding by making our CTA, Time Dependent. When the clock is ticking, and a deadline is in place people are less likely to put off the task.

When you were at school you most likely experienced this phenomenon; you had homework due next Tuesday, and even although you put it off until the Monday night, you still took action within that timeframe.

Therefore, give your audience a deadline by stating that you want them to act by a specific date.

End Summary & Action Point

To summarise, first you must identify the **Purpose** of your speech – what you are looking to achieve from both the audience and your own perspective. Once defined, create a **Call to Action** based on that purpose.

To make your Call to Action effective you must:

➢ **Position** it near the <u>end</u> of your presentation.
➢ Make the desired 'next step' **Achievable** and within your audience's control.
➢ Make it **Time Dependent** by including a deadline.

With that said, it's time to begin planning your next presentation. During your 15 minutes of action, think about a presentation you have coming up; it could be for work, in your personal life or anywhere in between.

Ask yourself, *"What is the purpose of this speech? What am I trying to achieve?"*. Once you have a solid answer to that question, consider what an appropriate 'Call to Action' would be. What do you want your audience to do next?

By doing this, you will uncover how you want to end your speech. From there, all you have to do is re-engineer. At first, this task may seem daunting. But once you identify the Purpose, momentum will build, ideas will spark, and you will find yourself enjoying the creative experience and producing your best possible work.

Share on Social Media

Please post your draft 'Call to Actions' online with the hashtag: - **#5PillarsPublicSpeaking**. If posted on LinkedIn and I see it, I will comment on your post with some helpful feedback.

Chapter 3

Part 2 - The Opening

Now that you know where you are going, your Opening becomes a lot easier to plan - because you have your End destination in mind.

Your Opening is undoubtedly the second most important part of your presentation. If you do not do or say something highly engaging and magnetic within the first 10 seconds, you run the risk of losing your audience before you've even begun.

You see, you need to earn your audience's attention; it will not just be given to you. In today's world, distractions are everywhere! People are obsessed with their phones, they want to talk to their colleagues, or they are debating in their minds what to have for lunch – Subway or Greggs? – it's a tough one!

So how are you going to interrupt this internal dialogue? How are you going to get their attention away from their phones? How are you going to bring them into the present?

This can be done by crafting an Opening which achieves two outcomes:

Context and **Curiosity**.

I call these '**The Two Cs**' and both are extremely important for creating an engaging and appropriate opening.

Context

Imagine you are sitting in an audience waiting for a speaker to come out on stage. Eventually she arrives and she is brilliant! Her body language is welcoming, her voice is dazzling, and she has the entire room in the palm of her hand. In her opening, she informs the audience that today they are going to look at the outer reaches of the galaxy and will aim to answer the age-old question; is there life out there?

You sit up in your seat, looking forward to the information you are about to lap up! But then the presentation takes a surprising turn – the speaker begins to talk about a different age-old question; which came first, the chicken or the egg? And this continues, as the speaker spends her entire hour weighing up the arguments of the chicken vs the egg. Now, she is a good speaker; engaging, funny and has fantastic delivery. But let me ask you this. If you were at that presentation, would you think something was off? Would you be slightly disappointed? Would you be annoyed if you had paid money?

Unless you have a strong opinion on the chicken vs egg debate, the answer is probably yes. This is because the speaker promised you one topic in her Opening and gave you an entirely different topic in her presentation.

I share this fictional story to illustrate a point; **Context** is important for setting your audience's expectations.

You need to give the audience an outline of what you intend to speak about. Think of this like a movie trailer – a 30 second film trailer gives you a rough idea of what the film will be about, and based on that knowledge, you decide whether you will see the film or not. It can be the same for your presentations.

Now, you do not need to tell them everything - in fact, I would even recommend being vague to create mystery. For example, if I was doing an Opening for the contents of this book I may say, *"Today I am going to share with you the 5 key skills you need to know in order to master any presentation,"*. Notice that I do not tell the audience what the 5 key skills are; I just vaguely refer to them. The trick is to say just enough but not too much.

Curiosity

The other important element to creating a captivating opening is to build a strong sense of Curiosity in the first 10 seconds. You need to say something which makes people want to hear more.

There are many different techniques you can use to create Curiosity. Here are some suggestions:

a) Rhetorical Question

Asking a rhetorical question is without doubt one of the most simple but effective techniques in public speaking. When you ask the audience a question, you momentarily control their inner dialogue; you make them think about what you have just said as they form their own answer in their head.

One of the most famous examples of a rhetorical question occurred when Sojourner Truth delivered her speech at the Women's Convention in Akron, Ohio in 1851. While stating her case with regards to why women should have equal rights she can be quoted saying,

'Look at me! Look at my arm! I have ploughed and planted, and gathered into barns, and no man could head me! And ain't I a woman? I could work as much and eat as much as a man - when I could get it - and bear the lash as well! And ain't I a woman?'

When creating your rhetorical question for your Opening, you obviously must relate it to the topic. I would also recommend choosing a question which the audience is unlikely to know the answer to as this will pique their interest.

b) Intriguing Statement

At my full-day public speaking workshops, I encourage attendees to practice delivering their speeches in front of the other participants as it's a safe environment where they can receive quality feedback and gain experience. I distinctly remember one nervous, cautious young man coming up to the front, placing his notes on the lectern and then looking out at the small group...

"784,500.... By the end of this presentation you will know why that number is ESPECIALLY important."

From that moment on, he had the entire room's attention; because we all desperately wanted to know what the importance of that number was. He created Curiosity, by making an intriguing statement.

You can also do that by saying something which is counter-intuitive, sharing a startling statistic or by revealing only a small part of your information – like the young man did at the workshop.

You're still wondering what the significance of that number was, aren't you?

c) Interactive Activity

A unique way of engaging your audience within the first 10 seconds is to get them involved inside the first 10 seconds. During a presentation I delivered at a university to 300 students, I opened by saying,

"Right, I want to start by asking you an extremely important question. And that question is, by a raise of hands, who here likes a shoulder rub?"

67

The audience sniggered and some people raised their hands.

"Fantastic, you are going to love today, and if you don't like shoulder rubs – trust me – you will in the next few minutes. I want everyone to stand up and turn to your right."

300 students stood up.

"Now, gently place your hands on the shoulders of the person in front of you and apply a small amount of pressure. Increase! Increase! Right go on – get in there – give them a good rub."

Laughter and discomfort filled the room.

"Okay, sit back down – now that you are loosened up, let's do some public speaking."

Out of the four techniques suggested in this section, the Interactive Activity will achieve the highest levels of engagement. The reason being, when you physically involve an audience, they must become engaged - as they have a part to play, instead of sitting idle.

Obviously, you don't have to go to the extremes that I did and have your audience rubbing each other's shoulders, but you could have them discuss a question, stand up and speak or engage in a game related to your topic.

There is however, one significant risk when implementing this technique; you could lose control of the audience.

If you do not present with confidence and authority, the audience may not take you seriously. I would recommend only using this technique when you have built up a good level of confidence in your speaking.

d) Meaningful Story

The wonderful thing about telling a story is that you can transport your audience from where they are to anywhere you want them to go!

I recently watched a fantastic speech online by leadership coach, Ryan Estis. He opened his speech by sharing a story about how a coffee changed his life. He was travelling back home for Christmas, but his spirits were quite low as he had just received some bad family news. However, a chance conversation he had with a very enthusiastic, caring barista changed his outlook. This conversation challenged his beliefs and encouraged him to consider how he was showing up for life and whether he was truly giving it his best. After engaging the audience with his story, Ryan was then able to bridge the gap by educating the audience on how that story relates to leadership and how we can all learn from it, moving forward.

You can use this powerful technique too, by sharing an engaging story related to your topic that provides significant value and learning points for your audience.

One tip I would recommend for this technique is to keep your story relatively short; 2-3 minutes in length. Remember - the goal is to create Curiosity in your Opening before moving on. Do not linger too long.

Opening Summary & Action Point

Earn your audience's attention by creating an **Opening** which provides **Context** and **Curiosity** within the first 10 seconds. Never take your audience's attention for granted, you are competing with more distractions than you could ever imagine.

Make your opening 10 seconds count.

In your 15 minutes of action, I challenge you to make a start on your opening 10 seconds. Thinking back to the presentation you just created an Ending for, I now want you to create an opening which has this end goal in mind. Use **The Two C'S** for this Opening and practice delivering it out loud. This will help you evaluate how it sounds.

Share on Social Media

Post a video of your 10 second hook on social media by using the hashtag: - **#5PillarsPublicSpeaking**. If posted on LinkedIn, and I see it, I will happily give you some constructive feedback on your Opening.

Chapter 3

Part 3 - The Middle

We have our ending (**Call to Action**) and we know what we need to do in our Opening (**Context/Curiosity**) - now we need to focus on getting from point A (your **Opening**) to point B (your **Ending**).

When considering the middle portion of your speech it is important to take into account your audience's perspective. The legendary motivational speaker Les Brown once stated,

"When you speak in front of an audience, they always have three questions in mind: Who are you? What do you have? And why should I care?".

With that in mind, I would like to introduce you to a structure for the middle part of your speech which will strategically answer each of these questions and will help you achieve the results you are looking for.

The 'YES' Speech Structure

YES, stands for: **You**, your **Expertise** and lastly, your **Solution.** The end goal of any presentation is to inspire action. You want your audience to act on your words. To achieve that, firstly you need to find a way to make them buy into you as an individual. Then you must demonstrate your expertise by showcasing your value, before lastly, presenting your solution (e.g. product, service or big idea) in an eloquent and appealing way so that audience members say, *"YES, I want that!"*.

You

When you are presenting, you are selling. You are selling a product/service, an idea, a new way of thinking or a different direction for your staff. One of the most important principles in sales literature is to first build rapport with your prospect – the reason being, we are much more likely to buy from people we like than those we do not. Public speaking is no different. If you do not like a speaker, you are probably not going to listen to that speaker and you certainly will not take action on their words unless you are forced to (e.g. at school). Therefore, the question arises, "How do I get an audience to buy into me?".

The answer? Share your story.

Your Story

Sharing your story is an incredibly powerful way to encourage an audience to warm to you. The reason being, when you share your story properly, audience members are given the opportunity to relate to you as there may be parts of your story that are similar to theirs.

One of the main reasons we like people is because they are like us. Therefore, you can use your own unique story to build that sense of similarity which in turn will create a strong connection.

That said, I do see a lot of speakers doing this incorrectly. I am talking about the guy who says, *"Right, now a little bit about my background,"* and proceeds to share his CV. He'll say, *"I did 7 years there, 5 years there, worked for them for 3 years, only spent two months with them - but I don't want to talk about that - then I quit my job and started a business"*. Woohoo! The problem is audiences do not connect with CVs; they connect with people. Therefore, to build strong rapport, I would encourage you to focus on the following three key areas:

1. *Your Journey*

   Share specifically how you got to where you are today and how you became the person you are now. Did a conversation or life event push you in a certain direction? Was there a turning point in your life? Who are the people who have shaped you on your journey? Also, be sure to include the highs and lows of your journey. Yes, we want to hear about your successes, but your failures are important too. Everyone has faced a failure or setback at some point; by sharing yours you create another opportunity to connect.

2. *Your Reason*

Share with the audience why you do what you do. What gets you out of bed in the morning? What is your 'why'? If people can understand your reason, they will have a better grasp of who you are as a person and the character of your intentions. Furthermore, people tend to share the same reasons; money, having a better life, their family or making a difference. If you share what drives you, the audience will be able to better relate to you.

3. *What You Have Learned*

Throughout your journey, you will have learned many different lessons. Some of these lessons may have come out of hardship and failure – learning what not to do. Others will have been obtained through success and victory – something that worked so you continued to do it. Share these lessons with your audience and look to impart value to them. Give your story a key message that people will remember and benefit from. Stop looking to immediately take and instead, look to give.

'You' Summary

By including these three key areas in your story, you will give the audience a very open and authentic view of who you are as a person and what it would be like to do business with you. Always remember - people buy into people first.

Expertise

You have achieved strong rapport with your audience – they like you as an individual, but now the question is; do they see the value in what you provide?

The next step is to showcase your expertise to your audience so that they buy into what you do. If you are a graphic designer, this is convincing people that you can design beautiful printed materials. If you are a life coach, it is persuading people that your methods really do make a difference. If you are a manager of a team, it is presenting the new strategy you intend to implement and convincing your team that it will work. This is a critical step, because if the audience do not see the value in your expertise, they are unlikely to respond when you deliver your Call to Action.

After working with many business owners on their pitches, keynotes and team presentations, I have found four key methods to be particularly effective for demonstrating the value of your expertise. We are now going to explore each of these methods. As we do, please consider the types of presentation you deliver as that will help you decide which method will work best for you.

1. The Unconventional Case Study

I think we have all seen case studies in presentations; they are boring, usually irrelevant, and often involve PowerPoint slides crammed full of tiny text that no-one can read. Believe it or not, firstly, case studies are not actually the problem and secondly, they do not have to be presented like that. The key to delivering an excellent case study that grabs peoples' attention and gives you credibility is to, at first, not make it a case study.

Imagine for a second that I am a digital marketing consultant; my speciality is generating leads for you via social media and Google. When presenting my case study, I would first say to the audience,

"I want you to think back to when you first started your business. Remember all the initial challenges; branding, expenses, establishing credibility, and of course, on top of all of that - finding work to pay the bills.

Just imagine how different that time could have been if you had 30 hot business leads on day one. How much easier would it have been to find work and get your business off the ground?

That is exactly what I did for one of my past clients; he started his business in September 2019, and two weeks later he already had his first 5 paid clients etc. etc."

The unconventional case study works by first presenting the information as if it is happening to the audience in front of you. You are enabling them to imagine what the results you achieved in your case study would mean for their own business/situation. Now that you have their attention, you can then introduce your case study as proof that you actually achieved the results you described. This powerful method ensures your case studies have a real impact.

2. The Highlight Reel

This method involves showing your audience different visual images of work which you have completed in a bid to highlight your value and expertise. Obviously, this method does not work for all businesses, but it can be extremely effective for building constructors, property agents, graphic designers and product providers amongst others.

Nonetheless, it is important to make sure that each image has a story behind it which demonstrates different parts of your skillset. For example, instead of a graphic designer quickly showing a picture of a slick business card and then moving on, they could pause on that image and explain the process involved in reaching that design. They could explain that they sit down with every single client and spend time working out the design together instead of merely giving them a generic questionnaire.

By giving insight into the bespoke nature of their service, audience members will have a better understanding of how this graphic designer adds value and they will be more likely to enquire about their service.

3. Audience Interaction

You may remember we discussed earlier in this chapter that an 'interactive activity' can be a great way to open your presentation. This method can also be effective for showcasing your expertise; by getting your audience physically involved in your field of knowledge, they will have a better understanding of the value you bring.

I saw a great example of this from a friend of mine, a drama/theatre director called Stuart Woodland. He was delivering a presentation on how to overcome anxiety and build confidence and used the fear of public speaking for demonstration.

He opened this activity by saying,

"Right, here is the deal. Before you came in today, I placed a yellow sticky note under one of your chairs with an 'X' on it…".

Looks of confusion appeared on the faces of the audience.

"In the next few moments, I want you to look under your chair; because if you have the sticky note, you're going to come up to the front and deliver a 10 minute presentation on the meaning of life…."

The looks of confusion quickly turned into looks of terror. Stuart gave the countdown,

"Ready, steady, GO!".

People started frantically looking under their seats, hoping and praying not to see a yellow, sticky, piece of paper dangling from the underside. Eventually, the anxiety-fuelled searching stopped, and everyone took a seat. But no-one was owning up to having the sticky note.

"Who has it?" asked Stuart in a very stern tone.

"There is no point hiding, you will be found."

Nervous laughter filled the room. Still, no-one was coming forward. In a final bid Stuart said in his most tension-building tone,

"Right, I'm going to count to three…. One, two, three……. Got ya!".

Stuart started laughing, but the audience remained terrified and confused. He went on to explain that he had not put a sticky note under any of the chairs, but instead had performed this activity to demonstrate that anxiety occurs due to uncertainty. The audience members did not know if they would be speaking for 10 minutes or not; it was the uncertainty of the situation that spiked those feelings of dread. Heads started to nod as the penny dropped for the audience; they now understood the cause of their anxiety and were attentively waiting to hear what Stuart's solution would be.

In this instance, the key benefit of this activity was that Stuart was able to educate his audience by having them fully engrossed in the topic, simultaneously demonstrating his knowledge of the subject while piquing the interest of the room.

However, don't worry; you do not need to be as dramatic with your audience activities. Simply posing questions for group discussion, facilitating team activities, or having an open dialogue with your audience can also be effective in providing evidence of the value you can offer.

4. *The Explicit Value Offering*

The last and final technique involves you explicitly sharing hints and tips related to your field that can truly benefit your audience. I regularly employ this technique. If I am delivering a short presentation at a networking event or conference, I will always include tips relating to public speaking which my audience can use in their next presentation. The benefit of doing this is two-fold. Firstly, it demonstrates to the audience that I know what I'm talking about and gives them a taste of what working with me would be like. Secondly, if audience members use the tips, they will achieve results and will naturally want to learn more. This often involves them contacting me and enquiring about my services. Therefore, you are simultaneously demonstrating your expertise and are also generating yourself potential leads.

Often people are quite cautious about sharing tips related to their field because they believe they are giving away all their best secrets. But you must understand that in this information-rich age, people can simply find tips relating to your field with a tap of their phone. Highly successful entrepreneur and author Daniel Priestley says it best,

'You are not paid for information; you are paid for implementation,'.

Thus, think about your line of work and consider what tips you could share with your audience that will demonstrate your value and will make them curious to find out more.

'Expertise' Summary

Before moving on, consider the four methods we have discussed above and ask yourself, *"Which would work best for my presentations?"*

You might have lots of case studies to draw from, or you might just be getting started and have none at all. Your business might have highlight reels of visual images or your work could be very much invisible. Interactive games might be ideal for your presentations or depending on the environment, they might not be appropriate. Sharing tips might work perfectly for you or your industry might not allow it. It is unlikely that all four of these methods will work for you but there should be at least two which do. Test them out, assess your audience's reaction and make a decision going forward from there.

Solution

The audience like you and they can see the value in your expertise; now you need to persuade them that your solution is the way forward.

To clarify, your **Solution** represents your product or service, big idea or the desired course of action which you want your audience to take. It is closely related to, but does not encompass, your **Call to Action** that we previously described. The two can be distinguished by thinking of your **Solution** as the advert for your service (e.g. explaining how it works and what it would look like) while the **Call to Action** is your sales close (e.g. asking for an answer or providing a next step). As mentioned earlier in this chapter, you must accept and become comfortable with the fact that you are selling when you are presenting. Even if you do not represent a product/service, you are still trying to convince your audience to implement the knowledge you have shared in your speech. Consequently, in this final section you will discover how to make your audience buy into your product, service or big idea.

When it comes to persuasion you must consider one key question; why do people buy stuff?

Is it because it makes rational sense, will benefit their lives, or is it because their friends have it? Maybe, but most likely the purchase is driven by emotions.

People <u>want it</u>, so they <u>get it</u>, and then they <u>justify it</u> with logic.

Therefore, when constructing your presentation, you must angle your approach so that you first appeal to your audience's emotions and then justify your case with logic.

Appealing to Emotions

Over the past few years, I have developed a strategy to appeal to an audience's emotions which has worked extremely well for my clients and I, and I believe it will work well for you too. It is constructed in three steps: first you must **Meet** your audience, then **Explain** to your audience, before creating **Imagery** for your audience. Let's break this down:

Step 1 - Meet

You need to meet your audience on a level playing field. What are their current struggles? What are their pain points, worries and concerns? Verbalise these problems, make your audience feel heard and show them that you fully understand what they are going through. By doing this, you will build credibility with your audience and grab their attention, as they will want to know if you have a solution they need.

Step 2 – Explain

This is where you introduce your product, service or big idea and fully explain how it will work, what it will look like and how it will benefit the audience moving forward. Highlight to the audience how the introduction of this method will relieve the problems discussed previously in Step 1. Make your explanation concise but clear, then move to the final step.

Step 3 – Imagine

Make your audience imagine what it would be like if they were already using your product, service, or big idea. Describe to them a compelling image where their pain points fade away, where more opportunities come their way and how you will be with them all the way in helping them achieve their goals. If the compelling image you describe is in line with your audience's desires, they will want what you have.

Add in Logic

Finally, once you have your audience in this elevated emotional state, introduce the logical arguments. Bring out your tremendous testimonials, your dazzling statistics and wow them with the track record you have achieved. By doing this you will adhere to that old sales adage; *'People buy with emotions and then justify with logic'*.

Solution Summary

This is a very powerful technique; if you are in sales I can guarantee you will at the very least get more leads by doing this; if you are a business owner, more people will enquire about your service; if you are a manager, more team members will understand your vision and will follow your lead. By introducing your **Solution** near the end of your presentation, you can smoothly transition into your **Call to Action**.

Middle Summary & Action Point

During your speech you must find a way to get the audience to buy into you, your expertise and finally your solution. That way you answer the 3 vital questions every new audience has:

'Who are you?'; 'What do you have?'; 'Why should I care?'.

This will lead to you achieving more of your presentation goals and having a greater impact on your audience.

But it all starts with action. That is why your last action point of this chapter is to start planning your story. In your 15 minutes of action, grab a piece of paper and a pen. I want you to write down 3 headings:

1. My Journey
2. My Reasons
3. What I've Learned

For each of these sections, I now want you to write down an exhaustive list; bullet point all the key moments in your journey, list all of the reasons which drive you, and write down all of the lessons you have learned along the way.

Once complete, select only one point from each heading. In other words, choose the most significant part of your journey, your deepest reason and your most valuable lesson. You now have the skeleton of your story; look to develop it through practice and evaluation until you have a powerful story which gets the audience to buy into you.

Share on Social Media

Share the results of this story-creating exercise on social media by using the hashtag: - **#5PillarsPublicSpeaking**. If you have questions post them on LinkedIn with this hashtag and I will answer as many as I possibly can.

Putting It All Together

We have covered quite a lot in this chapter. I know it's a lot to take in!

To conclude, let me simplify the speech structure we have covered. In sequential order this is how your speech should flow to an observer:

#1 **Opening**

Start your speech with an opening that provides your audience with Context and creates Curiosity.

#2 **Middle**

Use the acronym **'YES'** to plan your middle. Start by <u>sharing **Y**our Story</u>, then transition into demonstrating the value of <u>Your **E**xpertise</u> before introducing <u>Your **S**olution</u> to your audience.

3# **End**

Finally, end your speech with a clear <u>Call to Action</u> for your audience to follow. This Call to Action should be based on the <u>Purpose</u> of your presentation. Furthermore, it should also be <u>Achievable</u> and <u>Time Dependent</u>.

I've seen some outstanding results from those who adopt this **Speech Structure**; from business owners attracting more opportunities than they could ever have imagined from a single speech, to clients finally finding their confidence to present.

Start planning your speech today, and you will be one step closer to achieving your speaking goals.

Chapter 4

CLARITY

I am not a gifted learner. I have dyslexia. I have always found academic work particularly challenging. I have found myself feeling completely and utterly lost many times in my life, especially during my time at school and university. I share this with you to make the point that I am not the only one. Many audience members struggle to follow information in presentations and the worst part is that they suffer in silence – I know this, because I did it too.

You can be delivering a presentation to your audience thinking that they are following your every word, while - in reality - they don't understand what you are meaning and, worst of all, they won't tell you! This can lead to mistakes being made, reductions in productivity and your message being lost, simply because there was not clarity in your presentation. It would be easy to blame your audience for not approaching you if they have concerns. But, as speakers, you must take full responsibility – it is your job to facilitate an environment where audience members feel they can approach you and clarify points. In a society where rates of low self-esteem have never been higher, the daunting prospect of putting up your hand and asking a question is often avoided.

However, there are strategies you can implement to create crystal clear clarity which will help your audience understand from your first word to your last.

In this chapter, we are going to cover 7 of these strategies; 4 of them can be implemented while preparing the content of your presentation, and the other 3 can be deployed while you are actually delivering the speech.

Clarity During Preparation

Here are four strategies which you can utilise while writing your presentation and preparing your slides which will make your information far more digestible for your audience.

1. Stories Over Facts

Human beings have been sharing stories with each other since the dawn of time. Storytelling was how we passed on information, learned how to avoid danger and built relationships with other tribes. This process has become ingrained in our minds and that is why, when we hear a story, we are likely to remember it.

In your presentation, consider where you could replace facts or statistics with stories that embody these key points of information.

Recently, at a networking event, I saw a sales trainer called Barry Clark share a business message which he learned from his one-year old Labrador puppy. He set the scene for us, describing how this small golden bundle of fur had changed his and his partner's lives for the better. He also described how extortionately expensive dog food was – so much so, that he decided to seek out a new, cheaper source of food for his canine friend. Initially, the dog seemed quite happy with his new, tasty meals. But as time went on, sheer terror descended. The puppy started whimpering in pain and developed large boils all over his coat and face. They rushed him to the vet, who diagnosed that he was having a severe allergic reaction to the new dog food.

Naturally, feelings of guilt and dread consumed the couple, as they waited anxiously outside the vet's surgery room. After four long, tense hours the vet finally emerged from his office with good news – the puppy was safe. Barry went on to explain that the key lesson he learned from the experience was,

"If it ain't broke, don't fix it".

Changing the dog food caused he and his partner tremendous stress and large vet bills – which wiped away any saving he made from the new food. If it ain't broke don't fix it.

That message is something you are likely to remember and fully understand. That's because the story provided an excellent example of the message in action. This makes the information far more digestible, instead of just stating the lesson with no real-world example. Think about the key messages you want to share in your presentations and what stories could you use to aid the understanding of those messages.

2. Focus on The Visual

Remember how in chapter 1 we discussed that 65% of the world's population are visual learners (Inc, 2017)? Alongside our descriptive gestures we can improve the clarity of our presentations by including more visual content. For you, visual content might come in the form of graphs, charts, pictures, videos, imagery, slideshows, flipchart illustrations or verbal imagery.

If your presentation is lacking in visual representations, audience members may find it more challenging to retain and follow the information you are conveying. Attempt to appeal to visual learners by making your chosen form of medium visually friendly.

For example:

➢ If you like to use PowerPoint – reduce the amount of text on your slides and include more pictures or infographics to illustrate your points.

➢ If you like to use a flipchart, colour code your messages so that your written words become visually easy to follow.

> ➢ If you just like to speak during your presentation, think about creating visual imagery for your audience; make them imagine, make them feel as if they are there with you.

Tap into those senses and your audience will be far more engaged and your message will come across loud and clear. In a nutshell, when creating, always focus on the visual.

3. Meaningful Numbers

Do numbers creep into your presentations? Numbers can easily cause confusion; potentially because they are a relatively new form of communication compared to storytelling or body language. Nevertheless, the key to making numbers understandable is to make them meaningful.

For example, if I said to you,

"A new app business is gaining 5 million new users per month and they are currently on track to make £600,000 in gross profits this year,".

What would that mean to you? I spoke about big numbers but I didn't give those numbers much meaning.

However, if I said,

"A new app business is gaining 5 million new users per month; that is the equivalent of the population of Scotland joining this app every single month. Currently, they are on track to make £600,000 in gross profits this year – to put that into context, only one other app in their sector is making more than that,".

All of a sudden, those numbers have meaning. Thus, when giving meaning to numbers try to make comparisons or draw on equivalents which your audience are already familiar with.

4. Simplify to Clarify

In order to avoid confusion and consequently losing your audience, there is one simple but effective question you can ask yourself, *"Can I simplify this?"*.

While creating your presentation, ask this question throughout the entire process. When choosing your content, case studies, stories and anecdotes ask yourself, *"Is there a way I can make that case study easier to follow?"* or *"Is there a different story that I can use which my audience will better understand?"*

If you use PowerPoint, while creating your slideshow ask yourself, for each individual slide, *"Could I reduce the word count? Could I include a picture instead? Does each slide transition into the next, seamlessly?"*.

By asking yourself these questions, you begin to challenge and push yourself to create your best possible work. Work, which is engaging, transparent and is easy to follow. Ultimately, putting in this extra effort is going to produce a far superior learning experience for your audience and a positive experience for you as a speaker.

Clarity During Your Presentation

You now have four excellent strategies which you can use during the preparation phase. But, what about on the big day itself? How can you achieve crystal clear clarity during the chaos of a live presentation?

We are now going to cover three key strategies which will allow you to do just that and will build upon the foundation of the previous four.

5. Relate to the Room

A major reason that confusion descends is because there is a gap between the audience and the information the speaker is conveying; the audience just can't quite understand how the information relates to them. You need to bridge this gap. That can be achieved by deliberately relating your content to the specific people who are present in the room.

I almost made a huge mistake a few years ago when I was preparing to speak to a school. Usually, my presentations are in front of business professionals and SME owners but on this occasion, I was asked to speak to 300 senior pupils at a local high school. Before each important presentation I deliver, I always ask my girlfriend to watch and give me feedback because she is great at giving me constructive points for improvement and telling me... well, when I am crap. I think everyone needs to hear that sometimes. So, the night before, I showed her the presentation. However, 30 minutes in she interrupted me and said,

"Kyle, you do realise you are speaking to kids, right?".

"Yeah," I replied, a little confused.

"So why are you talking to them like they have a mortgage, drive a BMW and coach football on Saturday mornings?"

With so little time before the main event, this was not what I wanted to hear. I was speechless!

"Seriously Kyle, you are talking about strategies, mindset and from the perspective of someone who is in business – kids don't care about any of that! You need to start speaking their language!"

She was absolutely right. If I had continued in that vein, that presentation would have been a complete disaster. So, with 24hrs to go, I made some radical changes; I stopped speaking about strategies and instead shared stories from when I was their age. I reduced my speaking time and made the presentation more interactive, including games and fun activities which would make them laugh and learn. But most importantly, I made my content specifically applicable to them, the current situations they were facing at school and future ones they were about to face in further academia or traineeships. These adjustments made the presentation a great success and I received glowing comments on the feedback forms from the pupils.

The key lesson is that you need to consider who is in the room and present directly to them.

There is no point sharing information which will help large organisations if you are speaking to SMEs. Likewise, there is no use sharing information which will benefit businesses if you are speaking to individual customers.

Think about who is in the room and tailor your presentation to their needs.

6. Encourage Practice

There is a great quote by Benjamin Franklin that says,

'Tell me and I will forget. Teach me and I will remember. But involve me and I will learn.'

It is all very well listening to words, but the magic really happens when action is taken. That's why it's a fantastic idea to encourage practice in your presentations.

In more or less every presentation I deliver on public speaking, I encourage audience members to come up, often off the cuff, and practise speaking to the audience. If I have just covered SEO in Body Language, I will encourage them to incorporate a genuine Smile, good Eye Contact and Open Body Language in their speech. This transforms the learning experience for the audience as it moves from being a classroom-based idea to having a genuine real-world application.

Consider how you could transition your content – from being a classroom idea to having a clear real-world application.

If you are a leadership coach, perhaps you could have your audience split into teams and perform tasks which will require leadership and teamwork.

If you are a financial advisor, perhaps you could encourage practice by facilitating an activity where audience members can calculate their future net worth.

If you are a dream therapist perhaps you can take your audience through a quick practical activity which will help them take control of their night terrors.

The point is, regardless of your industry or sector, everyone can encourage practice in their presentations. This will significantly aid the learning experience for your audience and will prompt them to put your ideas into action.

7. Check In

Last but certainly not least, one of the simplest yet most effective ways you can ensure clarity is by checking in. Quite simply, this means asking your audience members if they fully understand your ideas:

"Does that make sense to you?"; "Is that clear?"; "Do you have any questions?"

By asking questions like these, you give the audience an opportunity to raise any concerns.

One of the biggest mistakes I see speakers making is they assume that the audience is following them. The fact of the matter is, they are most often not. We live in a society today which fears being judged, faces crippling anxiety and depression, and does not want to appear 'stupid' at all costs. For this reason, audience members are very unlikely to raise their hand, while you are in mid-flow, and say, *"I don't understand…"*. Potentially, you could be leaving people behind without even knowing it.

That is why you must ask and give the audience an opportunity to raise their concerns which in turn will give you an opportunity to clarify points. This will lead to the audience and you moving forward together. Of course, even with a prompt question, some audience members will still not speak up. To avoid this situation there are two techniques you can use:

➢ **Humour** – One of the best ways to disarm an audience is to make them laugh. If you have them laughing, you will be building strong rapport and they will feel more comfortable opening up to you.

➢ **Expand** – When checking in, don't just stop with one question. If you don't receive an immediate response, expand further by stating, *"There are no stupid questions,"* or *"Please ask if you don't understand, because you probably won't be the only one,"*.

By expanding you are teasing the questions out of your audience and will have done everything you can to obtain a response.

Ultimately it is up to the audience to ask, but by facilitating a safe environment where questions are welcomed and celebrated, people are more likely to speak up.

Your Action Point

We have covered 7 effective strategies which will help you achieve clarity in your presentations. However, your action point for this chapter is to only use one of these strategies in your next presentation – **Check In**.

Ask your audience if they fully understand after you have covered key points in your presentation. In preparation, you may want to use your 15 minutes of action to identify key areas of your presentation which may require check-in questions. You can identify these areas from past experiences (what previous audiences have struggled to grasp) and your own intuition, assuming you have awareness of the complexities of your subject.

This strategy will make an immediate impact on the learning experience for your audience. Once you have successfully implemented this approach, choose another and include it too. Then another, and another, until you are using all 7 of these strategies in tandem.

The end result for you will be presenting with crystal clear clarity which will improve the experience for every audience you encounter and will help you achieve your presentation goals.

Share on Social Media

Show me your check-in question examples through using the hashtag: **#5PillarsPublicSpeaking**. If posted on LinkedIn and I see it, I will comment with my feedback.

Chapter 5

IMPACT

E verything we have discussed in this book so far has led us to this final pillar – **Impact.** As we mentioned earlier – we can judge the success of a presentation by whether people take action on our words or not. Having an impact will swing the balance of your audience's decision and will make them far more likely to adhere to your chosen Call to Action.

Defining Impact

Impact has become a bit of a 'buzzword' in the subject of communication; everyone knows it is important to have an impact, yet we don't tend to clearly define what that means. Therefore, for the purpose of this chapter we will define Impact as:

Making a lasting impression which inspires action.

With this definition in mind, Impact can be achieved by ensuring that your presentation includes three key elements: **Connection, Uniqueness & Inspiration**. Think of these three elements as part of a cycle – each one is connected to the other and flows in a circular manner. For the remainder of this chapter, we will explore each of these elements — uncovering the truth of how you can have a significant Impact on your audience.

Connection

When I was just 14 years old, I heard for the first time, one of the most impactful voices in the world. Although young, I was troubled at this stage in my life. I was having a difficult time at school, struggling with my studies and fitting in with my peers. Outside of school, things were not much better — my whole life revolved around football (soccer) yet my performances on the pitch were often subpar because of the anxiety I felt before and during the game. And when your self-confidence is fully attached to that outcome, happiness can be hard to come by. Combined with family issues at home, failure of exams and lack of friends, in the eyes of a 14-year-old, my life was a complete mess.

But, when I turned on my computer and heard this voice, a sense of hope filled my mind. This speaker spoke with a purpose, with drive and with empathy — it felt as if he generally wished the best for his audience and wanted them to achieve their goals. Even though the video I was watching was over 20 years old, filmed in a country I had never been to and featuring a man who I had never met — I still felt a connection to that speaker. I still felt as though the legendary Motivational Speaker, Les Brown, was speaking to me.

You may have experienced this too – it might be a speaker you see in person or online but when they speak, their message and style completely resonate with you. They might talk about a situation you have experienced, something you are currently going through or an ambition you have for the future - it feels like they are speaking only to you. That is the power of connection, and that connection is a driver for impact.

But how can you build connection with your audience? How do great speakers like Les Brown build that incredible level of rapport? Of course, techniques which we have already covered in Body Language, Voice and Speech Structure (specifically 'appealing to audience emotions') do play a significant part. However, the icing on the cake is a combination of:

➢ Mindset
➢ Language

(i)   Mindset

Speakers who have a strong connection with their audience tend to have one trait in common – empathy. They understand what their audience is going through and genuinely, unquestionably, want to help them improve their current situation.

One of the best examples of a speaker who has an empathetic mindset is Oprah Winfrey. Whether Oprah is speaking to one person on her talk show or thousands at a conference, you can feel with every part of your being that she genuinely cares.

This sounds simple and is an obvious necessity, however you would probably be surprised that most speakers do not have this mindset. Instead of looking to **give** to their audience, most speakers are looking to **take** from their audience. They want to make quick sales, promote their brand or 'look good'. Don't get me wrong, these are important points (except that last one) but they are all secondary to helping your audience. If you want to build a strong connection, you must develop an empathetic mindset – where your primary goal going into each presentation is to help the audience as much as you possibly can. Interestingly, often adopting and believing in this mindset will improve your personal goals for sales and recognition, as individuals are much more likely to approach and enquire about your services if they can see that you care.

(ii)   Language

Stemming on from the introduction of your new mindset, changing your language is also especially important. The term 'public speaking' is actually quite misleading. It suggests that the activity involves speaking to many people all at the same time. Physically this is true - but to build a strong connection, you need to do the opposite.

This means speaking to the audience as if you are directly addressing one person. When audience members talk about a speaker who has made a large impact on them, they often say, *"It felt like he/she was speaking directly to me,"*. This can only be achieved by using language which is singular and directly speaks to one person.

If the language is not singular, and speaks to many, (e.g. saying, *'Ladies & Gentlemen'*) audience members will be less impacted as the message is not being specifically directed to them.

Another common example of speaking to the many, is that speakers will address their audience with phrases like, *"you guys"*, *"we will"*, *"what do you all think?"*. Each of these phrases can be made singular, and therefore more impactful, by only addressing one person; *"you will"*, *"what do you think?"*, *"you"* rather than *"you guys"*.

The word *'you'* grabs attention – because audience members feel like the speaker is directly addressing them.

Alongside speaking directly, you also should consider the nature of your language. Often speakers tend to use phrases they would not normally use because they are speaking in public. For example, many speakers will say, *"Without further ado,"*. Do you really use this phrase when you are having a one-to-one conversation? Do you say to your partner, *"Without further ado honey, let's have dinner?"*. No – therefore don't use it in your presentation.

Your word choice needs to be conversational and fitting with your personality. If it deviates from this, the audience will sense a lack of authenticity and any connection you have built will be lost. The key message here is to not overthink public speaking; you are just having an exciting conversation with one person while many are listening.

Uniqueness

We always remember the speakers who truly have an impact on us – we can recite their names, the content of their sessions and the specific emotions we felt when we were in their presence. Connection, without doubt, has a part to play but being **Unique** is what helps these outstanding speakers become memorable and impactful. In a hypercompetitive world full of noise, big promises, and information coming from every direction, you need to find a way to stand out. Now, the tips you have obtained in this book so far will help in achieving this. However, on this occasion, I want to dive deeper into this topic of 'Uniqueness' and show you three strategies which will help your presentations stand out amongst the very best. The three strategies are:

- ➢ 100% You
- ➢ Break the Pattern
- ➢ Reach a Summit

1. 100% You

Most likely, someone in person or online will have told you this before; *'just be yourself'*. Their reasoning behind this advice probably was something like, *'because it will allow you to come across as authentic on stage'*. Am I close?

This rationale is not false, however there is a more important reason why we need 100% of you on stage. You must understand that your profession is not unique.

Need a lawyer? You can find 100 different options at a click of a button.

Need something printed? Off the top of my head I know 10 different graphic designers who can help. Struggle for motivation? - there is a sea full of Life Coaches on deck waiting to help you. Even niche professions like my own – Presentation Skills Trainer – is not solely mine. Nevertheless, at this point you might say, *"But I'm nothing like my competitors, my service is completely unique!"* And that might be true, but unless you have extremely good marketing, people will not know this unless they are already in business with you.

Human beings are quite simplistic creatures – we like to categorise information so that it is easier to keep track of. That's why when you hear someone say, *"I'm a travel agent,"* your mind immediately puts that person in the 'travel agent category' with all the others. The only way to break out of your 'category' and create a lasting impression is to bring something different to the table.

And that differentiator is **you.**

Your personality is what will help you stand out – you think, react and talk differently to anyone else out there. Of course, there are people who are similar but they are not quite you.

I was working with a client who was involved in property – she had multiple presentations coming up at property conventions and networking events. Now, you must understand that this lady is a character – she's funny, talks really fast, is sometimes borderline inappropriate but has great passion for what she does. That's why I was very surprised when I saw her speak for the first time with a monotone voice, zero humour and overall a very 'safe' approach. It was almost as though the fear of speaking was preventing her from being herself. This is common with many novice speakers. When the attention of the room is on them, they can get caught in the headlights. After the presentation I asked her,

"Emma, was that really you up there?".

She thought for a second, and then said, *"No, but I don't think I can be me,"*.

"Why?" I asked with surprise.

"Because, well, I don't want people to judge me."

I nodded in acknowledgement, *"Emma, it's important to remember, in public speaking, people will judge you anyway, so you might as well be yourself when it happens."*

She smiled and laughed.

"Seriously," I continued, *"you need to be yourself when you're up there, that is what makes you stand out,".*

She nodded, and we set about working on how we could make this happen. Two weeks later, I was at a networking event and Emma was the main speaker. However, this time things were vastly different. She was speaking with pace and energy, her Glaswegian humour was flowing, she brought up topics which made people raise eyebrows and then choke with laughter, her passion for her work came soaring through and above all, she was 100% herself. People were talking positively for days about Emma's presentation. So, when you approach your presentation, make a conscious effort to allow your personality to come through. Be 100% you.

2. Break the Pattern

If you want to be Unique, you can't act like everyone else. Winston Churchill's philosophy on speech writing was revolutionary,

'Tell them what you are going to tell them, tell them, then tell them what you've just told them.'

Simple but extremely effective – so much so, that everyone and their Nan, now delivers a speech in this pattern. It can be compared to the mobile phone – when they first came out in the 1980s, they were viewed as something special, revolutionary, and unique. You had to be 'somebody' to have one. But today, everyone has a mobile phone and they are no longer special and unique, just like Winston Churchill's technique.

Therefore, if you want your presentation to stand out you need to be willing to deviate from the norm. You must try something different; something people are not used to seeing or hearing, something that potentially could be risky. After all, the greatest rewards lie on the other side of risk.

This could be including an interactive audience activity, not using a PowerPoint, making a bold claim or attempting humour.

One of the greatest TED talks in history, by Ken Robinson was full of risk taking. Within the first 10 seconds he cracked a joke, then went on to explain how University professors are 'disembodied' only using one half of their brain, before arriving at his main, controversial point that schools are killing creativity. If coaches had seen Ken's talk written down on paper, many probably would have encouraged him to change his content, to take less risks, and to adopt the more universal TED talk style of click and point.

But Ken's risk taking is what made his talk unique, gained over 18 million views and be regarded by many as *'the best TED talk of all time'*.

If you want to be Unique your presentation must break the pattern. Don't be afraid to stand out, take risks and challenge conventional wisdom. **Remember, greatness lies on the other side of risk.**

3. Reach a Summit

What is said or felt last, **lasts with** your audience.

As discussed in previous chapters, this is why the end of your presentation is the most important part. Yet, in so many speeches the end is often the most boring part; speakers sum up what they have previously spoken about, if it's the Winston Churchill approach they tell their audience what they have just told them for a third time and there is a general feeling of winding down.

I would like to encourage you to go the other way. I want you to view the ending of your presentation as the **Summit** – the peak of your speech. As mentioned previously, you should have a direct Call to Action at the end of your presentation. As you get closer to this action point, lift the energy of the room; increase the volume and speed of your Voice, make your Body Language more dynamic and expansive, make your language direct and compelling as you propel towards your key message, and once you have your audience in that elevated state where they are fully engaged and waiting for your next words - deliver your Call to Action.

Reaching a Summit will benefit your presentation in two ways:

➢ firstly, because you are leaving your audience in an elevated state, they are much more likely to remember your presentation in a positive light. This can potentially lead to more opportunities, referrals or people approaching you for business.

➢ Secondly, because your audience is in a positive place, they are much more likely to act on your words. People tend to make decisions or take action when they feel encouraged. Use this to your advantage.

Inspiration

You have developed a strong **Connection** with your audience and your **Uniqueness** has shown through. The last required element which will help you make a significant impact is **Inspiration**. We have mentioned many times in this book that our goal is to get people to act on our words. But the only way to make that goal a reality is to inspire our audience in some capacity.

I am being very particular when I use the word 'inspire'. A lesson I learned from a very accomplished speaker coach of mine, called James McGinty, is that you never want to aim to 'motivate' your audience. You see, motivation is simply telling your audience what to do. It can work, but what is more effective is **Inspiration** – showing your audience what to do.

We see the effects of these two influences all the time. Often, motivation is what helps people get started. It's that short-term, energising feeling of limitless possibilities that encourages people to: quit smoking, lose weight, change their job, leave a toxic relationship or start a business. But when that motivation ceases, so does the progress that individual has made - as they are no longer being told what to do.

Inspiration is different. Yes, it encourages people to get started, it makes them all warm, fuzzy and positive, but unlike motivation, when that feeling dies down people do not simply stop. If they are truly inspired by what they have seen and heard, an 'idea' will stick with them forever. That idea is that, *'It is possible...'*

Whether it be making a change, overcoming an obstacle, or reaching a seemingly unattainable goal, that idea will remain and will encourage them to act. You want to know why? Because they have seen someone do it.

They heard a story, saw the evidence or gained information which made the task unquestionably achievable in their mind. This is what the best speakers do for their audience – they give them belief not by <u>telling them</u> but instead <u>showing them</u> the way forward.

115

We are now going to cover two techniques which will help you inspire your audience, both of which are linked back to information we have discussed in previous chapters. Hopefully, you see by now that all 5 Pillars are connected.

The two techniques are:

> Stories that Inspire
> Deliver with Conviction

1. Stories that Inspire

We know it's important to share your own story because one of the first questions people ask is, *Who are you?*".

But that is not the only story you should share. I would recommend you share other people's stories which will inspire too.

This point reminds me of a young man I encountered at a speakers club a few years ago called Jacob. He was shy, timid and when you shook his hand, he would barely look you in the eye. Nevertheless, he came to this club because he wanted to become more confident, and he wanted to improve his current situation. But on that first night, his confidence was absolutely shattered. We were practising impromptu speaking – which involved each of us receiving a question without prior knowledge of the subject and immediately having to stand up and speak on that topic for 2 whole minutes. This activity puts the fear into most, and it was apparent from his expression and tense body language that Jacob was feeling the pressure.

His question, *"Jacob, what was the greatest moment of your life?"*.

After a short applause Jacob found himself at the front of the room looking at 20 people he did not know, staring directly at him. Ten seconds passed by... Jacob remained silent, 20 seconds passed... his lips began to tremble, ... 30 seconds passed – the audience didn't know what to do; whether to intervene or let Jacob continue.

But by the time 40 seconds had passed, Jacob uttered two words;

"I'm sorry."

He sat back down.

I didn't see Jacob for a while after that as I was travelling, however when I returned to the club, I witnessed something extraordinary. Jacob was delivering a 7-minute speech, entitled – *'The Greatest Moment of My Life'*.

I took a seat and waited for Jacob to begin. And when he did; he stole the show! He had the audience mesmerised with his energetic body language and powerful voice. He had them laughing as he shared stories from his past, present and potential future. Finally, he had them standing as they gave him a much-deserved ovation for the message he had delivered.

You see, during the speech Jacob explained that the greatest moment of his life was that 40 seconds of silence. Because that time made him realise that he needed to find his voice. You must understand that Jacob grew up in a family who didn't value his voice and therefore strictly encouraged him to remain silent. Naturally, this had an impact on the rest of his life as communication has always been a skill he feared.

That's why Jacob's speech was so inspiring; because it symbolised him breaking past his limiting beliefs and finding the power in his own voice. Jacob reminded the audience, just like I will remind you now, that you too, can do this! Regardless of your past fears or current situation, you can find the power of your voice. It takes practice and patience but most importantly, action. In Jacob's own words,

"If I can do it, you can do it too,".

Even though you don't know Jacob, you can still relate to his story and be inspired by it.

You see, what an inspiring story does, is it dismantles an individual's current beliefs about what they are capable of, then reassembles those beliefs with the added knowledge that 'it is possible'. This comes about because you have learned that someone else has overcome the same adversity you are currently feeling. That spark of knowledge is what will encourage your audience to take their first step and stay the course.

2. Deliver with Conviction

My first tip on Inspiration was very much based on the content of your presentation. But as we already know, that is only half of the equation in public speaking since we need to consider Delivery – and I want you to deliver with **Conviction.**

So often I see speakers deliver points and information without appearing as if they honestly believe what they are saying. As a speaker you must act as a leader – the audience are following your lead whether you like it or not. If you present without conviction, passion or belief in your ideas, the audience will reflect those feelings when you ask them to act. That is why it is critical that your delivery is on point.

Of course, we can use some of the previous techniques we have learned to convey belief in our ideas. Using the Body Language acronym of SEO (Smile, Eye Contact & Open) will indicate to your audience that you are confident in your ideas and transparent with your intentions. Using the Tone of Certainty or Excitement will display your passion for the topic and will help you present your all-important Call to Action with conviction. Most importantly, the combination of both Body Language and Voice will keep your audience fully engaged and will show that you actually care for them, their current situation and making their future better.

Ultimately, that is what we look for in a leader – someone who wants the absolute best for their people and truly cares about making a difference. So, deliver your message like you mean it, say it with conviction and passion, truly have the best intentions for the people in the room and you will find that your audience will reflect that when it comes to taking action.

Summary

To have a significant impact on your audience the three key elements you need are:

Connection, Uniqueness & Inspiration.

You have to **Connect** to your audience so that each individual member feels as if you are speaking directly to them. You must be **Unique** so that people remember your name, what you said, and what you stand for. Finally, you need to **Inspire** your audience so that action is taken consistently, long after you leave. If you include these three elements in your presentation you will make a lasting impression which inspires action.

Your Action Point

It's time to start speaking directly to your audience. Replace non-direct phrases like '*Ladies & Gentlemen*', '*You guys*' and '*Without further ado*' with more natural and direct language. Speak as though you are having an exciting conversation with one person while others are in the room.

Talk using your everyday language and use the word '*You*' repeatedly. To practice this, use your 15 minutes of action to run through key parts of a presentation you have coming up. Pay close attention to how you address your 'imaginary audience' and if appropriate, change your collective phrases into singular ones. Once again, recording yourself will help with this process.

Once you have integrated this language adjustment, consider the other factor in **Connection**: mindset. Once this element is complete move onto **Uniqueness** and then **Inspiration**. The key here is to take a small step. Do not try everything at once but do take that first step.

Share on Social Media

Post your recordings on social media using the hashtag: - **#5PillarsPublicSpeaking.** If you would like my insights on your clips, share them on LinkedIn with the hashtag and I will comment with constructive, positive feedback.

Chapter 6

BECOME WATER

*E*mpty your mind, be formless, shapeless — like water. Now you put water in a cup, it becomes the cup; You put water into a bottle it becomes the bottle; You put it in a teapot it becomes the teapot. Now water can flow, or it can crash. Be water, my friend.'

This quote from Bruce Lee (Enter the Dragon) captures the essence of what we must strive to achieve when speaking in public and in life.

You see, when we stand up on stage some variables are controllable – such as what we will say if pre-planned, and some variables are not – such as how our audience will react. Now remember, it is the audience we are there for – we want to inspire, educate, entertain or even sell to them. Thus, they are the centre focus of our presentation – a situation which isn't actually the best scenario, when you think about it.

Ideally, as speakers, we would want the centre focus of our presentation to be something predictable - something which is consistently the same every time we encounter it. That way we could prepare a message that hits the mark on each occasion because we know what we are walking into. The problem is, in public speaking, you never really know what you are walking into. Audience members might be in a positive state of mind; happy, energetic, and enthusiastic or they might be in a negative state of mind; upset, angry and anxious. Or most commonly – they might be indifferent.

One of the biggest mistakes novice speakers make is that they do not recognise this unpredictability. They go in and continue with one form of presentation regardless of the reaction they receive from their audience. They are not being 'water' - they are just being the 'teapot'.

The point is that when you are presenting you need to be willing to consistently adapt to the different scenarios you find yourself in. That means utilising the full range of the **5 Pillars** we have explored in previous chapters to address your audience appropriately.

In this penultimate chapter, I want to show you how you can use all 5 Pillars in tandem while also adapting to the different situations you find yourself in.

Utilising All Five

By now, you have probably realised that the 5 Pillars we have covered are not separate but inter-connected.

To convey confidence, you need open Body Language and a tone of Certainty in your voice while being '100% you'.

While sharing your story you should consider using the structure of your 'Journey, Reason, and What You've Learned', while also relating that information to your audience (Clarity) and delivering with conviction (Impact). Even when it comes to delivering your key message, you need synergy in all five techniques to deliver the best possible result.

At this point I would love to show you how to use all 5 Pillars together for the Opening, Middle and End of your presentation. But I won't.

That would assume every presentation is the same and we know that this simply is not the case. So instead, to be as helpful as possible, I will show you how to use the 5 Pillars appropriately depending on the type of audience you encounter.

The 3 Different Audiences

For the purpose of simplicity, I have narrowed down the possible types of audience you can encounter into 3 distinct groups: High, Low and Indifferent.

High Audiences

By the way, if you need to laugh every time I say 'high audiences', that's fair enough – you'll have a good time.

A High Audience is the best type of audience to meet. This group are enthusiastic, very attentive and genuinely want to be there. If you hold your own workshops, conferences or webinars where people willingly attend, you will most likely find that your attendees fit this profile. These individuals are also open minded and do not dismiss information without first giving it a chance.

So how should you react when you stumble across this gem of an audience?

First, let's evaluate the situation; these people are already on your side, they see the value in what you do and they just want to learn as much as they possibly can.

Reviewing the 'YES Structure', I would place less emphasis on getting the audience to buy into 'You'. You still need to share your story, but you can spend less time on this and focus on other areas.

Likewise, when it comes to your 'Body Language' and 'Voice' you do not need to be super expansive or dynamic – the energy of the room is already 'high', so there is no need to take it to the stratosphere unless that is part of your gig.

Even with 'Clarity', adaptations can be made. Since the audience is attending your speaking event willingly, there is a possibility that they are already familiar with much of your work. If that is the case, there is no need to clarify every single point you make as you would with an audience who has never experienced the topic before.

So that's what you should pull back - but what should you emphasise? Out of the 5 Pillars here are my top five picks for this audience:

1. **Eye Contact (Body Language)**

   A high energy audience naturally wants to build a connection with you. Allow them to do so by using prolonged Eye Contact which makes them feel fully addressed.

2. **Tone of Mystery (Voice)**

   This audience are already extremely interested in what you have to say. Make them become even more enraptured by building tension and anticipation with the Tone of Mystery, before revealing your key points.

3. **Focus on Solution (Structure)**

   Rarely do you have people in the room who immediately see the value in your expertise. This is one of those occasions where you do, so take advantage of that by focusing on the 'Solution' part of your 'YES' structure. These people want to take the next step with you.

4. **Encourage Practice (Clarity)**

> These individuals want to upgrade their skillset in your area of expertise. Give them the opportunity by allowing them to practice the skills you teach on the day. It will be an experience they will learn from and will appreciate.

5. **100% You (Impact)**

> This audience want to see you. They like you and respect you – give them the best version of you.

Unless you have a huge personal brand or have a great reputation for your events, audiences like these are few and far between. However, when they do come along, enjoy the experience, try new things out and pay them back by providing as much value as you possibly can.

Low Audiences

This is the most challenging group you will encounter. They do not want to be there. They have minimal interest in your subject and in some cases, are actually rooting against you.

Audiences can be in this negative state of mind for several reasons; stress about their current situation, anger due to the way they have been treated, fatigue due to the time they have been listening or they could just generally be closed-minded – not wanting to change. If you do in-house training for companies, work in education or are involved in politics you will most likely come across this type of audience at some point.

So how do you break past this negative energy and get a 'Low Audience' on your side?

Obviously, some of the skills that we have learned are not going to be the most helpful in this situation. For example, this type of audience is already less likely to act on your words. Now, that doesn't mean that they won't, it just means you have to adjust by placing less emphasis on your 'Solution' from the start and instead focus more on building rapport and credibility first.

Likewise, when it comes to Impact, being '100% You' is always good – but the audience aren't keen on you in the first place. So, you need something else to break past that barrier. Even when it comes to essential skills like Interaction, you need to be careful how you first engage in order not to fall flat on your face.

Personally, when I meet this type of audience, I focus on these 5 points:

1. **Open (Body Language)**

   It is especially important that you convey to the audience that you are not a threat and are instead a friend. Furthermore, holding this strong posture will also show that you are not intimidated and deserve respect.

2. Understanding/Certainty (Voice)

It would be a disservice for me to pick one Tonality here. You need to express Understanding so that you can break down the barrier between you and the audience. Furthermore, you need Certainty in your voice to convince the audience that your way forward is correct.

3. Focus on 'You' (Structure)

Focus all of your energy on getting this challenging audience on your side. Remember action does not take place unless they buy into you first. Tailor your story so that it resonates with the specific people in the room.

4. Relate to the Room (Clarity)

The more time you spend directly talking to your audience, discussing their situation, their problems and making your information relevant to them – the more likely they are to listen, as you are being helpful.

5. Break the Pattern (Impact)

This type of audience has seen hundreds of click and point presentations and are not impressed. It's going to take something special and risky to flip the script. Take this opportunity, do something different and earn the respect of the audience who aren't sold on you, just yet.

Facing this type of audience can feel very intimidating and, if you let it, can spike your anxiety. However, it also represents opportunity; a chance to do something special which will test your confidence, ability and will to succeed.

Worst case scenario, you learn a lot about yourself. Best case scenario, you elevate yourself.

Go for it!

Indifferent Audiences

This last group represent the majority of audiences you are likely to face. In general, these people have nothing against you but, they are not overly pleased to be there either. They don't really have a strong opinion on your topic and probably have no idea who you are. If you speak at external conferences, networking events or have to deliver training to an external team, you will most likely encounter this type of audience on a regular basis.

Now the good news is that this audience is the easiest to influence; in other words, they can initially be indifferent to you, but 10 minutes in, you could turn them into a 'high' audience. Likewise, you could also convert them into a 'low' audience. The point is that this audience is open to positive persuasion – they don't have any fixed ideas, points of anger or a desire to hijack your presentation. It is up to you as the speaker to transform them from not caring to being fully onboard and engaged with your content.

Believe it or not, this book was designed with this type of audience in mind. Every single technique listed in these pages will work, if performed correctly, for this audience. Nevertheless, to focus your learning, here are my top 5 picks from each chapter:

1. Smile (Body Language)

You need to take this audience from 'not caring' about you to loving you. One of the best ways to suggest you are friendly, approachable, and confident is to Smile. It's disarming, and when people smile back that will calm your nerves too.

2. Excitement + Speed (Voice)

The energy levels of this audience are flat. In order to build engagement and make people become emotionally invested, you need to lift the energy. Do this by speeding up your voice to build momentum and by using the Tone of Excitement to transfer your passion to the audience.

3. Opening (Structure)

The 'YES' structure will work extremely well with this audience. However, I would encourage you to focus on nailing your Opening. Practice saying something in the first 10 seconds which will intrigue your audience and will make them want to lean in. If your start is good, you will be good.

4. Stories Over Facts (Clarity)

Right now, there is a gap between you and this indifferent audience. Bridge that gap by conveying your technical information through stories that the people in the room will be able to relate to.

5. Language (Impact)

Speaking to the masses will keep this audience switched off. You need to speak to the audience as if you are directly addressing one person. Think about your word choice, make your audience think by asking daring questions or making statements. Speak to one and you will reach them all.

When preparing for a presentation I would encourage you to anticipate that your audience will be 'indifferent'. That way when you do encounter those blank faces who do not care about you and have no idea what you do, you will remain calm as you are already prepared to face this challenge. Even if you arrive and the audience is not indifferent, but instead is 'high' or 'low', you will still be in a good place to adjust and will not have to make drastic changes. Therefore, prepare for the 'indifferent' to give yourself the best chance of success.

Summary

Of course, it is important to plan for a presentation. But it is important to plan to adapt as well. An 'indifferent' audience can quickly turn into a 'high' audience, and a 'high' audience can easily turn into a 'low' one through a simple mistake or a throwaway comment that you thought might be funny.

As I mentioned before, in public speaking you don't know what you are walking into, and to add to that, while presenting in the moment, you still won't 100% know what you're about to go through. But that is what makes public speaking exciting, dynamic and truly fascinating. No two presentations are completely identical, each one has its own unique challenges, highs and lows, and unforeseen events.

Embrace this fact, enjoy the controlled chaos and above all: *'**Be water, my friend**.'*

Chapter 7

YOUR NEXT STEP

Together we have been on a journey. One which started with direct promises, bold claims, and advice on where to go when the zombie apocalypse hits. This was followed by the 5 Pillars, which introduced us to 'macho man', 'speed' loving presenters, chicken vs egg debates and 'High Audiences' to name but a few highlights. We have now arrived at that critical point in our journey; the point in a speech where you need to lift the energy of the room, reach a Summit, and deliver your all-important Call to Action.

We have reached the end.

My biggest hope is that this journey does not become a waste of your time. When I say that I don't mean, "*I really hope you like the book,*"; rather, I hope you take action on this book. I have mentioned this throughout, from the first chapter to now the very last:

'The success of a presentation can be determined by whether your audience act on your words or not'.

Do you remember the action points from all five chapters? Here they are in chronological order:

1. **Body Language**

    Start to introduce 'SEO' into your next presentation. In other words, practice <u>Smiling</u>, holding correct <u>Eye Contact</u> and displaying <u>Open</u> Body Language.

2. **Voice**

    Out of 'TTV' (Tonality, Tempo, Volume), your first step is to include changes of <u>Volume</u> in your voice. Attempt to include 'Spikes' in your next presentation by lifting your Voice at the start of sentences.

3. **Structure**

    Begin constructing your next presentation by focusing on defining three key areas:

    ➢ Your Call to Action
    ➢ Your 10 second Hook
    ➢ Your Story

4. **Clarity**

    In your next presentation 'check in' with your audience by confirming that they fully understand your point before moving on.

5. Impact

Focus on speaking directly to your audience through specifically concentrating on your word choice. Remember the word 'You' is one of the most powerful lexicons we have in language.

Notice that for each of these action points I have <u>not</u> asked you to act on the whole chapter; just a small, achievable step which you can take. But it gets even better, because moving forward I do not even want you to act on all five of these action points. All I ask is that you act and focus on one, <u>singular point.</u>

Your 15-minutes of action has given you a taste of all 5 action points. My question is, which one did you struggle with most?

Whatever the answer, I want you to take a step in <u>that</u> direction. If you don't know how to portray confidence, focus on SEO. If your voice is dull, concentrate on spicing it up with Spikes of Volume. If you struggle with Structure, Clarity or having an Impact, narrow your aim so that you hit the action point for that specific area.

Attack your weaknesses and they will eventually become your strengths.

Moving forward there is no point trying to do everything because that will lead to you doing nothing. Save yourself time, energy, and emotion by taking your next step towards achieving that one, singular action point.

Final Thoughts

I want to close this book by sharing with you a personal story. Recently, I've been doing a lot more running. In fact, in the past 10 months I have run 1,173 miles to be exact. I have been training for and participating in Marathons and less well-known races called Ultramarathons – which is any significant distance over 26.2 miles.

I do not do this because I like to run; actually, in some ways, I strongly dislike running. But one cold, hard fact remains. The more I do it, the stronger I become mentally. I am able to endure more, stay calm in challenging circumstances and be resilient no matter how many times life puts me down. However, on October 6th, 2019, I had none of that and I was in serious trouble.

The landscape looked like a picture postcard of Scotland. Beautiful dark red heather had taken over the ground while the magnificent mountains and hills controlled the sky, standing tall and proud as they waited patiently to see the carnage which would soon unfold. One thing which you do not see on Scottish postcards, is the relentless, soul-destroying rain and wind.

3,584 runners were being battered by gale force winds and soaked to the bone by the driving rain. We were waiting at the start line of the Loch Ness Marathon – one of Scotland's biggest running events of the calendar year.

As I wiped the rain off my brow for the 700th time, I thought to myself, *"Well, there is no turning back now"'*. This was my first ever marathon and I could not wait to get started. I had been training for months, had become well acquainted with stomach testing energy gels, and felt ready to run the race of my life.

However, as I was waiting, I became a little distracted. You see, there was a seasoned runner standing next to me, and he was putting something all over his body – massaging and caressing himself. My curiosity was spiked. Naturally, I decided to just stare at him. Eventually, he noticed my looks of bewilderment, turned to face me, and said something I will never forget,

"Big man, have you vaselined your nipples?"

"No, have you?" I cautiously replied. Then he looked me straight in the eye and said in a voice which could rival a foghorn,

"I've vaselined everywhere, pal!".

BANG! Thankfully at this point the race gun went off and Vaseline Man crusaded off, slipping and sliding past all the other runners. Feeling shellshocked and even more bewildered, I set off too.

One of the good things about the Loch Ness Marathon is that the first few miles are all downhill. When you combine that with the 'buzz' of finally starting this epic journey, many runners decide to throw caution to the wind, and go for it.

I was no different; I was slaloming past my fellow runners with a big smile on my face. I was finally doing it - I was finally running a marathon!

Even the sun was beginning to break through the dark clouds. I was feeling positive, confident, and alive. As I hit the 3-mile mark I looked down at my watch and, to my astonishment, I had just ran my last mile in 6 minutes 15 seconds. I had never run that fast during training, not even close! Was this just my race day pace or would I pay for it later on?

People run marathons for many different reasons; some do it for a charity, the challenge, the memories, to travel, to compete – some even do it for the goodie bag. I was doing it for redemption.

You see, in April of that year I was not feeling like myself. Like many, I had ambitious goals coming into the New Year; I wanted to become the World Champion of Public Speaking, I wanted to start making significant profits with my small business and I generally wanted to feel as though I was making progress with my life. So far, these plans were not working out.

With the World Championship, I was knocked out during one of the earlier rounds of the contest, not even making it close to my dream of reaching the international stage. But more pressingly, I was not getting anywhere with my business. I had read all the books, attended the seminars, taken action but the money and opportunities were just not coming in. I felt like I was hitting my head off a brick wall – I was going nowhere.

When I started my business at age 22, I visualised myself crushing it – hosting sold-out workshops, travelling to speak all across the country and beyond, and achieving a good income which would allow me to live the life I wanted. But instead, no one was coming to the workshops, no one was asking me to speak and barely anyone was paying me.

If you are a business owner, or know someone who is, you will understand that a person's business is an extension of their self. They have poured everything into it; their time, energy, passion, money – everything they have got, a full commitment. Consequently, when that business is failing, their confidence and self-esteem go down with it.

I was beginning to question everything; was I cut out for this? Was I good enough in the first place? Was everyone else right, should I just have got a 'real' job? Doubt plagued my mind as I didn't know which direction to turn. Those close to me were supportive, but the fact remained – I was failing.

Luckily, in the midst of this difficulty I came across a book called *'Can't Hurt Me: Master Your Mind and Defeat the Odds'* by David Goggins.

This book captures the life story of an ex US Navy SEAL who overcame an enormous amount of hardship, achieved unbelievable physical feats and developed a mindset to help others to do the same. The way I took it, the essence of the book is that the more physically uncomfortable situations you put yourself in, the stronger and more calloused your mind will become.

At this point, I needed some of that. So, I thought of the most uncomfortable situation I could imagine – running a marathon - I signed up to the race closest and started training. As much as it was about strengthening my mind, it was also about proving to myself that I could achieve something significant.

As I passed mile 10, I reminded myself of that fact. The course was more uphill now which brings its own unique challenges. But I was relishing the challenge, seeing every hill as an obstacle which would make me stronger. Quietly I was thinking to myself, *"Vaseline Man, I'm coming buddy!"*.

However, as Oscar Wilde said, *'Expect the unexpected'*. Just 3 short miles later I was feeling vastly different. Pain was starting to invade my legs as they throbbed with every step. This forced me to slow down, and the frustrating thing was all the other runners around me were somehow able to speed up. They were effortlessly gliding by as I was left panicking and disoriented in their wake. But the worst part was when I realised that I wasn't even halfway through the race. I had heard about people hitting the wall and the pain which came with marathons. But really – this early? That same doubt I had about my business was now beginning to creep into my race – did I have it in me to make it to the end?

I think we all have doubts at some point. With a focus on public speaking, perhaps you have doubts about your ability to speak articulately, whether you will be able to withstand the pressure of a live audience or if your message has merit in sharing. What I've learned is that the only way to move past that festering doubt is to act. Staying in your own head and thinking about all the potential cataclysmic problems which could occur will not help you. Taking action will bring your mind into the present and will give you the opportunity to move forward.

That's what I discovered at mile 13, the power of focusing on the next step. I realised I had to stop focusing on the other runners around me and also stop thinking about how far I had to go. Instead, I needed to solely concentrate on putting one foot in front of the other at my own pace, much like you should do with your speaking.

The pain was still there but, step by step, I was getting closer to my goal. One step of progress eventually turned into 2 miles, then 5 and then 7 – I had made it to mile 20!

The end was well and truly in sight with just 10km (6.2 miles) left to go. For the first time in a while I told myself, *"You can do this!"*.

At that point something miraculous began to happen – the pain started to retreat! I was able to speed up again. I felt like a car which had finally found its correct gear – I was racing down the course – wind behind me, sunshine above and feeling full of belief.

Many runners refer to this surge of energy as a 'second wind' – I didn't care what it was called, all I knew was that I was devouring this course like a Domino's Pizza Two-for-Tuesday deal. Then, just when my energy, momentum, focus, and belief were at an all-time high, I felt sheer agony.

It was my right leg. The front of my leg (the quadriceps) started violently spasming and contorting and then completely locked out straight like a steel bar. So that you fully understand this; right now, straighten your own leg and point your toes up towards yourself – that was the position my leg was locked in – and no matter how hard I tried to bend it and regain control, it was not moving. I limped to the side of the road with a look of both dejection and sheer misery on my face. I wanted to sit down to try and rest, but because my leg would not bend, I was unable to. Waiting at the bottom of a steep hill, I watched as what felt like hundreds of runners passed me by. Yes, they were all suffering and battling their own difficulties too, but they were still moving. With five miles left to go, I was in trouble.

Have you ever had a goal, but then something happens – hits you out of the blue – which makes you question it?

Often when in pursuit of achieving success, in any field, the unforeseeable manifests itself right before your eyes. In public speaking such manifestation might come in the form of your audience not reacting in the way you hoped, your PowerPoint cutting out, you feeling ill or down prior to speaking, or you might just freeze in the moment – standing there, fully exposed, in front of a room full of strangers with no idea what to say next.

Unfortunately, I must be honest and tell you that one of these things, if not all of these things, could happen at some point as you are pursuing your speaking goals. You won't be able to control when it happens or who it happens in front of, but you will be able to control what happens next - whether you give up and stop your pursuit or stand up and take that next step in the right direction.

This has happened to me on many occasions during presentations, and as I was standing at the side of the road at mile 21, I knew this was exactly what I needed to do. After 15 minutes of feeling sorry for myself, wishing I were somewhere else, and doing a lot of moaning, I finally summoned the courage to take that next step.

The 5 miles which followed were horrifically challenging. The pain had fully conquered my legs, the rain started pouring down once again and the miles ticked by, so slowly. Literally, every step at this point was a victory.

But, with just 1 mile left to go, I saw something shimmering in the distance. What was it? A bird? A plane?

No, it was Vaseline Man!

Despite his extensive race day preparation, I could tell he was suffering.

I caught up with him – and as we ran side by side, we both started laughing. We had started this race together, now we were on the verge of finishing it together. The last 50 metres were nothing short of extraordinary; crowds of people had gathered and were cheering us on, the race officials proudly called out our names on the PA system as we got closer and closer, and as the finish line came into view, a surge of energy coursed through us both as we crossed together. Moments after, Vaseline Man turned to me with big open arms and a beaming smile as we went in for a big hug.

Despite feeling his slippery chest against mine, I have never felt a greater sense of absolute euphoria in my life as when I reached 26.2 miles.

You see, in that moment I realised what I had been doing wrong with my business and personal goals. I had been focusing all of my attention on what I could not control. I was allowing my happiness to be dictated both by unforeseen external events and by where I currently stood in relation to my long-term goals.

If this race taught me one thing, it is that the only thing you truly can control is your next step. It was solely concentrating on my next step which got me through the challenging moments of that race. And it was taking those small, achievable, courageous steps which allowed me to prove to myself that I could achieve something significant.

You too can achieve something significant; you too can achieve something great.

But it's up to you to take that next step in the right direction.

There is an old Chinese proverb, which states that: *'The journey of a thousand miles starts with a single step'*.

Choose your action point from this book, put your time, energy and effort into that one singular step, then take another, and another, and another and before you know it, you will have made a marathon's worth of progress with your public speaking.

It is absolutely up to you - put in the work, be courageous in your pursuit, and have your end goal in mind.

It all starts with that small yet powerful first step — take yours today!

REACH OUT

Thank you for reading *The 5 Pillars of Effective Public Speaking*. I hope this book has inspired you to plan and pursue new, outrageously ambitious speaking goals. If you would like further assistance with these fresh, exciting goals, Kyle can help in a number of ways:

One-to-One Training

Working with you individually on your upcoming presentations by offering personal feedback and support to help you hit your targets.

Team Training

Helping your team present more effectively in their high-stakes presentations so that they engage potential customers and secure more sales.

Conference Speaking

Delivering unbelievably impactful keynotes to your delegates which will cause immediate action to be taken. Kyle can even deliver his '5 Pillars' keynote at your conference.

Membership

In October 2020, Kyle will be launching a membership programme that will bring together individuals who have the common goal of enhancing their presentation skills. It will include tailor-made, monthly webinars amongst other benefits to support members.

For further information on all these services and more, please visit Kyle's website: www.confidencebydesign.co.uk. Leave an enquiry message and you will receive a response within 48 hours.

Connect on Social Media

Kyle frequently shares extra public speaking tips on his YouTube channel and LinkedIn profile. Connect today to start the conversation.

LinkedIn: https://www.linkedin.com/in/kylemurtagh/

YouTube: https://www.youtube.com/c/KyleMurtagh

REFERENCES

Ekman (1992)

https://www.paulekman.com/wp-content/uploads/2013/07/Facial-Expressions.pdf

Ekman, P. (1992). An argument for basic emotions. *Cognition & emotion*, *6*(3-4), 169-200.

Inc 2017

https://www.inc.com/molly-reynolds/how-to-spot-visual-auditory-and-kinesthetic-learni.html

Printed in Great Britain
by Amazon

54814510R00095